101 TOUGHEST INTERVIEW QUESTIONS

101
TOUGHEST
INTERVIEW
QUESTIONS

...AND ANSWERS THAT WIN THE JOB!

DANIEL POROT AND
FRANCES BOLLES HAYNES

REVISED

TEN SPEED PRESS
Berkeley

*This book is dedicated to the thousands of people who shared with us
their genius, originality, enthusiasm, and knowledge about how to
answer and react positively to the toughest questions they were asked
in interviews. We are thankful to all of them.*

Copyright © 2009, 1999 by Daniel Porot and Frances Bolles Haynes

All rights reserved.
Published in the United States by Ten Speed Press, an imprint of the Crown
Publishing Group, a division of Random House, Inc., New York.
www.crownpublishing.com
www.tenspeed.com

Ten Speed Press and the Ten Speed Press colophon are registered trade-
marks of Random House, Inc.

Library of Congress Cataloging-in-Publication Data
Porot, Daniel, 1941–
  101 toughest interview questions : —and answers that win the job! / Daniel
Porot and Frances Bolles Haynes. — Rev. ed.
      p. cm.
  Summary: "A list of 101 commonly asked job interview questions with sample answers, plus interviewing tips and strategies"—Provided by publisher.
  1. Employment interviewing I. Title. II. Title: One hundred and one toughest
interview questions. III. Title: One hundred one toughest interview questions.
  HF5549.5.I6.P67 2009
  650.14'4—dc22

                            2009018652

ISBN: 978-1-58008-849-7 (pbk.)

Printed in China

Cover design by Michael Kellner
Text design by Colleen Cain

10 9 8 7 6 5 4 3 2 1

First Revised Edition

CONTENTS

LIST OF QUESTIONS

Concern #1: Can You Do the Job?

1. What interests you most about this job?
2. What do you think this job will offer you?
3. What did you like most and least in your last job?
4. How many people have you supervised at any given time?
5. What financial responsibilities have you had?
6. What is the most difficult decision you have had to make in the last twelve months?
7. Which of your achievements has given you the greatest satisfaction?
8. Do you think you are underqualified for this job?
9. Would you be willing to undergo psychological testing?
10. What have you learned from your previous jobs?
11. In your last job, did you discover a problem that your predecessors had left untreated?
12. What type of job is best suited to you: staff or management?
13. What do you see as the major trends in our field?
14. Why do you think you have the potential for this job?

15. Do you think you are overqualified for this job?

16. How would you describe the position for which you are applying?

17. How do you improve yourself professionally?

18. What are your greatest achievements?

19. How would you describe your ideal working conditions?

20. Are you looking for a limited or unlimited time contract?

21. What would you do if you were completely overwhelmed with work and knew you couldn't meet the deadline?

22. Do you prefer to work alone or in a group?

23. How do you learn best?

24. Do you think job security exists anymore?

25. I have three candidates, including you, for this position. What criteria should I use to decide who to hire?

26. How much time will you need on the job before you are fully productive?

27. How does an employer demonstrate social responsibility? Does this matter to you?

Concern #2: Who Are You?

28. So?

29. Tell me about yourself.

30. What makes you unique?

31. How do you respond when your ideas are rejected?

32. What kinds of things cause you to lose interest in a project?

33. What do you like to do when you are not working?

34. How do you react when you realize that you have made a mistake?

35. *Silence.*

36. How do you react when you are angry?

37. How do you operate under stress?

38. What regrets do you have about your career?

39. Don't you trust that we will follow through with this agreement?

40. What are your strengths and weaknesses?

41. What do you most want to improve in the next year?

42. Can you give me some examples of your creativity on the job?

43. How would you describe your personality?

44. How do you react when you are told your methodology isn't working?

45. How do you define success?

46. What is your leadership style?

47. What is your favorite website and why?

48. Who has been the biggest source of inspiration in your professional life, and why?

49. What is your work style?

50. What are your future ambitions?

51. What do you think of my style of interviewing? If you were conducting this interview, would you do something differently?

52. How did you overcome the negative impact of losing a job?

53. What is your biggest failure and what did you learn from it?

54. What are your weaknesses and your limitations?

55. Describe your ideal job and employer.

56. What are your long-term professional goals?

57. How would you respond if I told you that your performance today has not been very good?

58. What type of decision is the most difficult for you to make?

59. Could you describe your worst day and how you dealt with it?

60. Are your past actions consistent with your values?

61. What will bring you the most satisfaction in your next job?

Concern #3: Will You Fit In at the Company?

62. How long will you stay with us?

63. How would you describe your last boss?

64. How do you contribute to team spirit?

65. Why were you let go from your last job?

66. How do you think your subordinates perceive you?

67. Describe the most difficult person with whom you have worked.

68. Would you like to sit in my chair one day?

69. How would you characterize your relationships with your colleagues?

70. What types of people do you have the most difficulty dealing with?

71. Can you discuss a time when you had a disagreement with your last boss?

72. Describe the best boss you've ever had.

73. If your boss implemented a plan or policy that you strongly disagreed with, what would you do?

74. How would you rate the last company you worked for?

75. How do you deal with office politics?

76. Please discuss a career decision you made that was questioned.

77. Why do you think communication is important at work?

78. What is your teamwork style?

79. What was the outcome of your last performance evaluation?

80. Why are you looking for a job?

81. Why have you been unemployed for so long?

82. Why did you quit your last job?

83. Why do you want to work for us?

84. What is the status of your job hunt?

85. Have you approached other organizations?

86. Why should I hire you instead of someone else?

87. If I were to make you a firm job offer, what would your answer be?

88. Have you gotten any job offers?

89. How will you decide which job offer to take, including ours?

90. We're just about done. Do you have any questions to ask me?

Concern #4: What Will You Cost Us?

91. What was your last salary?

92. Are you willing to lower your salary expectation?

93. How did you justify your salary in your last job?

94. At this stage in your career, why aren't you earning a higher salary?

95. What are you worth?

INTRODUCTION

Not many people like to be surprised, surprisingly enough! Most of us prefer to know what we're getting into so we can prepare ourselves. This holds true for things good and bad. Even happy occasions like surprise birthday parties can throw people off balance. We aren't comfortable with events and circumstances out of our control, so it's no wonder that most people get nervous when they think about interviewing for a job. We fear what will happen if we don't perform well, especially because our actions and behavior in this brief encounter can profoundly affect our future.

The good news is that we can take measures to minimize the fear and dread associated with interviewing. By preparing ourselves for what is likely to happen, we can replace our feelings of discomfort and anxiety with calmness and confidence. We wrote this book to help job hunters familiarize themselves with commonly asked interview questions so they can begin the process of formulating appropriate responses. Of course, not all of these questions will be asked in every interview, but it's a safe bet that you'll hear a fair number of them. When job hunters contemplate what they might be asked, put together thoughtful, well-reasoned answers, and then practice delivering these answers, they will perform much better during interviews and increase their chances of being hired.

Preparing well for an interview enables you to respond exactly as you intend and to impart exactly the information you wish to impart. When the playing field is fairly level and there are many similarly qualified candidates, an employer may choose someone else over you because he or she is more qualified or better suited to the company culture; however, you never have to lose your chance at a job again because you did not prepare adequately. Like everything in life, interviewing for a job is a skill that requires practice. Even with natural talent, opera singers, actors, and major league pitchers all work hard to perfect their craft. Being good at whatever you undertake demands preparation and dedication.

In this day and time, it's hard to imagine that anyone would set foot into an interviewer's office without considerable preparation. Yet, in what can be one of the most crucial and future-shaping activities we face—interviewing for a job—people often proceed blindly, with little preparation. It is easy (and costly) to assume that the skills required to perform a job are the same skills necessary to interview well for that job. A person can be a highly skilled engineer or a superb marketing manager, but if she lacks the ability to convince an interviewer of her competence and skills, she will likely lose the chance to get the job for which she is best suited.

To interview successfully, it is essential that you know what information interviewers need from you to make their decision, and you must be prepared to offer it easily, without making them dig for it. Chapter 1 deals with this topic in depth, discussing the kind of information interviewers are trying to gather during their discussion with you. Interviewing well also requires a plan that balances different response approaches so you can make the best possible impression at every turn. In chapter 2, we explore these strategies and how they can make an interview interesting and successful.

Knowing what kind of questions you will likely be asked makes all the difference in your attitude and confidence as you approach your interview. With that in mind, we present the 101 toughest interview questions you can expect to encounter, and provide sample responses on the reverse side of the page for each question. Do not merely memorize the answers and spout them back verbatim to an interviewer; instead, use them as jumping-off points to start thinking about how you can answer the question in a way that reflects who *you* are. As you read the questions and responses, carefully think about your own experiences and skills and formulate an answer that is specific to you. If your answers sound "canned" and don't ring true to you and your experiences, an interviewer will likely pick up on this and think that you are dodging the question. Good interviewers will keep asking the question in different forms until they get what they think is an honest answer from you. The bottom line is, giving "canned," impersonal, or untruthful answers will do more harm than good.

As you consider each question in this book, write down concrete examples from your professional life to help you create a response that is uniquely yours. If one of the sample answers applies to you or your experience, you may want to use it as a basis for your answer and then expand on it, tailoring it to reflect your particular qualifications or history. Some of the sample responses will not apply to you; if so, do not run the risk of using any of them to answer a question. The best answer is one that allows you to provide specific information and examples that best reflect who you are and what you can do.

Instructions

As you anticipate potential questions that you might be asked in an interview, read through the 101 questions (but not the sample answers) and select those that would be the most difficult or challenging for you to answer. Any question that you dread being asked is one that you should prepare for thoroughly—take extra time to contemplate your response and then practice delivering it confidently and articulately. If you fear a specific question or type of question, always make time to deal with it *before* you are sitting across from the interviewer. You don't want to be in the position of struggling to answer a challenging or uncomfortable interview question, especially if you were fairly sure it would come up. Be ready to tackle the hard stuff—gaps in your career, problems with bosses or coworkers, whether you are overqualified or underqualified, why you left your last job, and so on. You can't stop the interviewer from asking these questions, but you can diffuse your anxiety by being ready.

Once you have made a list of the questions you find challenging, write down an answer that you might give to an interviewer for each one (but don't look at the sample answers yet). After you have written down your responses, go to the question and read through the sample answers. Select one or two answers that you like best, then see how they compare to your own. Choose the answer that best fits you and your situation, then practice your response until you are comfortable and sure you will remember it. If your answer is significantly different from the sample responses, check with trustworthy people who know you well—friends, relatives, present or past coworkers, and so on—to see how they respond to your answer and if they have any constructive feedback to offer.

If you can, engage the help of a friend or family member when preparing for an interview. Ideally this other person will be preparing for an interview as well, but if that isn't possible, pick a trusted friend or family member with whom to practice your responses. Try the following exercise together:

1. Sit down and face each other.

2. Select five to fifteen questions per person. You may choose the questions randomly or pick those that you most need to practice.

3. Each person takes a turn at being the interviewer and the candidate. Every time an effective answer is given, jot it down; later on, memorize it for future use in an interview.

4. Once you're finished, discuss all the questions and the best answers. It is always a good strategy to double-check your responses with others who know you well (the more the better) to ensure that each is the best possible one for *you*.

A Note about the History of This Book

It's hard to believe that we first wrote this book over ten years ago. In that time we have seen an absolute proliferation in the use of the Internet as a job-hunting tool (whether for good or bad remains a topic for another day!). It's more important than ever before to arrive at an interview knowing a good deal about the company and the job tasks and being well prepared for the questions that may be asked. Both interviewers and job hunters are more savvy now, and interviewers expect much more from candidates, knowing there is an abundance of resources to help them prepare and impress. The sheer number of people applying for any single job can be staggering, and this heightened level of competition allows interviewers to be far more critical and selective.

The nature of typical questions has also changed, although many of the tried-and-true questions still remain staples for most interviewers. To keep pace with these changing trends in job hunting, we have revised the questions in this new edition—we've deleted those that felt outdated and added new ones that are more relevant to today's marketplace and work environment. We have also updated and added more sample responses to most of the questions, in the hope that they will resonate with many people and provide a solid starting point.

chapter

1

Understanding the Interviewer's Concerns

To ace your job interviews, you need to understand the role of interviewers and what they are trying to accomplish. Sure, they want to hire someone for the position, but they want to hire the *right* person. It is their goal to make an informed and reasonable decision, so every question they ask has meaning and importance. The questions they ask aren't random; they don't pull them out of a hat and hope that they can divine who is the right person for the job. Every question is designed to illuminate and clarify some piece of information about you so they can determine whether you are the best person to hire. In the broadest terms, every question asked in an interview addresses at least one of the following four main concerns:

1. Can you do the job?

2. Who are you?

3. Will you fit in at the company?

4. What will you cost us?

7

Understanding the subtext of a question can help you customize your responses so you provide the needed information and remain a viable candidate. We have organized the 101 questions into these four concern categories, although many questions could fit into several (or all) of these categories. For instance, an interviewer might ask you, "What is your leadership style?" to find out about the outcome of your previous leadership experiences ("Can you do the job?"), your character traits ("Who are you?"), or how you interact with others ("Will you fit in at the company?"). How you respond will determine how the interviewer interprets and uses the information. As you will see, there is certainly some overlap across the categories; however, it's best to focus on what information the interviewer needs from you rather than which category a question belongs to!

Concern #1: Can You Do the Job?

Do you have sufficient experience, training, education, aptitude, and interest to be productive? Can you deliver what the organization needs from this position? How has your background prepared you for this job? What have you achieved up to now? What do you know about this job and company?

In most interviews, the majority of questions asked are to determine whether you can actually do the job for which you are interviewing. If your answers do not clearly demonstrate that you can do the required tasks, you will likely not be considered a serious candidate for the job. Many questions that assess the extent of your qualifications are of a highly specific nature, differing from job to job and industry to industry, and so are not appropriate for this book. Make sure you are prepared for any job-specific questions that you could be asked. For instance, if you are interviewing for a highly technical job, be ready for technical questions!

For a complete list of questions that address the interviewer's first concern, see pages vii–viii. The primary strategy for dealing with this type of question is to provide concise and concrete information. Be sure to:

- Answer with conclusive and clear-cut information.
- Offer facts, figures, and statistical proof to support your claims.
- Provide examples of your skills and abilities.
- Discuss your past experience, summarizing the tasks you can do and have done.
- List your strongest skills.
- Describe your accomplishments in detail, including outcomes of successful projects, proposals, and so on.
- Outline your relevant knowledge.
- Describe your education and training.
- Illustrate your decision-making skills.

Concern #2: Who Are You?

What do you like and dislike? What are your main characteristics and traits? What is your personality like? What are your values and goals?

In addition to determining whether you can do the job effectively, interviewers want to know who you are. No interviewer will make a decision to hire you unless he or she has a sense of who you are as a person, what you care about, and what motivates you. This information can be even more critical to interviewers than knowing whether you meet every qualification. If they can't get a sense of the "real, authentic you," they will not consider you seriously for the job.

For a complete list of questions that address the interviewer's second concern, see pages viii–x. The primary strategy for dealing with this type of question is to provide positive and truthful information so you can give the interviewer a "window" into your personality. Be sure to:

- Answer with passion.
- Share your activities and interests.
- Focus on job-related issues when appropriate.
- Describe personal achievements and offer examples of personal growth.
- Talk about your goals and values.
- List your best characteristics and traits.
- Suggest an exchange of ideas about a job-related subject.

- State any negative information quickly and briefly and move on to another topic immediately.

Concern #3: Will You Fit In at the Company?

Will you be part of a problem or part of a solution? How do you relate to others? How have you gotten along with others in your past? What do you expect from us? How interested are you in working here?

Most employers have had at least one bad experience in the past when hiring someone; they need to know that they won't be making a mistake by hiring you. You must make interviewers feel that the risks to them are very minimal if you are hired. Specifically, you need to reassure them that you will fit in at the company, get along with your coworkers, actively contribute to the company's well-being and progress, and not add to the challenges that they already face.

For a complete list of questions that address the interviewer's third concern, see pages x–xi. The primary strategy for dealing with this type of question is to provide information about how you have reacted in the past and to show there will be no unpleasant surprises from you in the future. Demonstrate that you get along well with others and can relate to people at all levels of the company's hierarchy. Be sure to:

- List your interpersonal skills and describe methods you use to deal with people.
- Give examples of your interactions with former superiors.

- Talk about teams you have worked with and the tasks you accomplished together.
- Share positive comments others have made about you.
- Discuss other people (such as former colleagues, bosses, or clients) only in positive terms.
- Describe how you maintain strong communication within your professional environment.
- Show how you have overcome difficulties or challenges in the past.
- Explain why you want to work for them.

Concern #4: What Will You Cost Us?

How much will hiring and employing you cost the company? What do I need to offer in order to get you? What are you willing to trade off in order to work here?

If an interviewer can satisfactorily address the three preceding issues and is interested in you as a potential employee, the fourth issue then becomes relevant. An interviewer will only address the cost issue seriously if you are a viable candidate for the job. However, some interviewers may bring up the subject of salary early on to test the waters and find out whether your expectations are compatible with their budget. It's usually a mistake to answer any salary question with a specific dollar figure, especially during the early stages of an interview, when the job responsibilities and tasks not have yet been well defined.

For a complete list of questions that address the interviewer's fourth concern, see pages xi–xii. The primary strategy for dealing with this type of question is to delay discussion of salary until all other issues are settled satisfactorily for both the interviewer and you, the candidate. Once that is done, you must show the value of your contribution. Be sure to:

- Research salary figures for the job beforehand.
- Postpone discussions about salary until there is a thorough understanding of the job responsibilities.
- Do not move to negotiation until a definitive job offer has been made.
- Do not be the first to mention a specific salary amount.
- Discuss salary ranges rather than specific amounts whenever possible.
- Ask questions for clarification and define any vague terms.
- List the benefits of value you will accept.
- Make sure that you and the employer agree on what constitutes the entire compensation package.
- Never lie about past compensation.
- Describe specific accomplishments to illustrate your worth.
- Link the responsibilities of the job to your value.

chapter

2 **Formulating Your Responses**

Understanding an interviewer's concerns enables you to provide appropriate, useful answers to the questions asked of you. Along with practicing your responses, knowing what information the interviewer needs from you will allow you to approach your interviews with strength and confidence. Keep in mind that every answer you give will tell the interviewer something about you—even remaining silent says something! Some responses are more effective and appropriate than others—depending on the situation, timing, and personality of the interviewer—so it's important that you determine the best strategy to use for the question at hand. Be sure to maintain a balanced approach by using different strategies throughout the interview. For instance, you don't want to make a joke of everything, but neither do you want to appear so serious that the interviewer wonders if you have a sense of humor at all. You don't want to provide lengthy, elaborate answers to every question, but neither do you want your answers to be too brief or simplified.

Consider the following fifteen strategies as you contemplate how to respond to specific questions.

1. First and foremost, listen!
2. Provide the most relevant information.
3. Rephrase the question or ask for clarification.
4. Answer carefully or avoid answering altogether.
5. Communicate more than one thing with your answers.
6. Don't volunteer personal information.
7. Be concise.
8. Lose the adjectives—stick with facts and figures.
9. Reassure your interviewer.
10. Use humor when appropriate.
11. Be honest—it's still the best policy.
12. Control your body language.
13. Keep it professional.
14. Smile, relax, and look happy.
15. Ask great questions yourself.

1. First and Foremost, Listen!

Don't be in such a rush to prove how bright you are that you don't actually listen to what is being asked. It's easy to jump ahead in your mind and assume that you know what the rest of the question will be, particularly when you are nervous or anxious about how you will respond. You'll end up so busy preparing and rehearsing the answer in your mind that you won't really listen to the interviewer. Listen carefully until the interviewer is through asking the question, then take an extra second or two to collect your thoughts before answering. You won't be judged harshly if you do this; in fact, you might earn a few brownie points if you provide a thoughtful answer to what was actually asked.

Be careful not to overlook those two-part questions either. Oftentimes an interviewer will ask a question about a certain situation or behavior and then tack on "Why?" at the end. It's this "Why?" that tends to get neglected in many candidates' answers. Make sure that you fully address the "Why?" so your answer is complete. If you aren't sure you've done that, ask the interviewer, "Did I answer your question?"

2. Provide the Most Relevant Information

It's a great strategy to think to yourself every time you are asked a question, "What if this were the only question I get to answer?" Pretending that you have only this one question will help you give the most pertinent, useful information to convince the interviewer that you should get the job. When interviewers say, "Tell me about yourself," what they really mean is "Tell me about your *professional* self." You might think it's nice to tell them where you were born or what your favorite hobby is, but save that for another time—that kind of information probably won't influence their decision about whether or not they should hire you.

Every time you answer a question, ask yourself, "Is the information I am telling the interviewer going to help him or her decide to pick me for this job?" Make sure the answer is yes.

3. Rephrase the Question or Ask for Clarification

Not every question you are asked must be answered immediately. Sometimes it's reasonable to wait to respond, particularly when this brief delay will clarify exactly what kind of information the interviewer is seeking. If a question is very general or vague, you can say, "Could you please be more specific?" or "I'd be happy to answer that, but first may I ask you _____?" Some interviewers will purposefully be vague in their wording to see how you will respond. If that happens, you can either rephrase the question to make sure you fully understand it or you can ask a follow-up question for clarification. It's better to take a slight detour than to head in the wrong direction by hastily answering a question that wasn't asked.

4. Answer Carefully or Avoid Answering Altogether

Some questions are better left unanswered altogether, but handling this properly can be tricky. If you're faced with a tough question that you know is dangerous to answer, try to avoid answering by using humor or suggesting another topic to discuss before returning to the question. For example if asked, "What are you worth?" you might remain silent for a moment and then respond, "My career path is important to me, and decisions influencing its direction are not based primarily on financial concerns. Therefore, perhaps I can address this question after we have discussed my qualifications further." It's okay to duck one or two questions creatively, but don't do it more often than that or the interviewer might think that you are hiding something. Take these difficult questions very seriously and think carefully about how to respond.

5. Communicate More Than One Thing with Your Answers

Use your answers to provide the most information that you can, yet do so succinctly. In some of your answers, it might be wise to talk not only about your job skills but also highlight positive personal characteristics or achievements. You can discuss your education, past experience, transferable skills, and interpersonal traits in combination—this kind of summary quickly helps the interviewer get to know you better.

6. Don't Volunteer Personal Information

Resist the temptation to offer up too much personal information. It's usually a mistake to talk a lot about yourself or your life outside of the professional realm, particularly in a first interview. Some information is considered off limits for interviewers to ask about (although they may ask these questions anyway), but don't volunteer personal information that interviewers know they can't legally ask for but *love* to have. Don't mention your kids or your parents or how you spend your Sundays. Avoid sharing any information that does not relate to why you are the strongest candidate for the job.

7. Be Concise

Keep your answers short—they should range from about thirty seconds to two minutes (for more technical questions). If you go on for longer than that, you risk losing the interest of your interviewer. Most interviewers will let you know what they are interested in by the follow-up questions they ask. When you've said something that catches their attention, they will probe for more information.

When you practice what you want to say ahead of time, you can prevent yourself from rambling on in the interview or even worse, seeming unprepared. For example, if asked, "What interests you most about this job?" you can respond by mentioning three key tasks of the job that you would enjoy.

8. Lose the Adjectives—Stick with Facts and Figures

Anyone can offer a self-description full of flattering adjectives, regardless of whether they're true or not. You can say, "I am competent, motivated, reliable, and enthusiastic," but so what? How can you prove it or measure it? Using adjectives to describe your work and yourself is offering only *subjective* data.

The best way to describe your skills and qualifications is to cite *objective* data. Describe who you are and what you have accomplished with concrete examples that use facts and figures. If you say, "I am great at raising money," it doesn't have the same "pop" or persuasive currency as if you say, "Last year I raised 1.2 million dollars in revenue selling our two top products." Adjectives weaken your case. Let your achievements and the corresponding results speak for you. The interviewer can then decide if you are "competent, motivated, reliable, and enthusiastic."

(Of course, the exception to this rule is if an interviewer asks you to list three adjectives to describe yourself! Then go ahead—but be honest; don't just say what you think the interviewer wants to hear.)

9. Reassure Your Interviewer

It is your job to reassure interviewers that the risk in hiring you is minimal. Describe one or two past achievements to show job skills and responsibilities you have mastered, using examples with facts, figures, and tangible proof. For instance, if asked, "Why do you think you have the potential for this job?" you might respond by mentioning your three strongest qualifications that correspond to the job duties and responsibilities.

10. Use Humor When Appropriate

Sometimes a little humor can lighten the mood and put people at ease. If you're asked a question that lends itself to a humorous response, go ahead and try one. Humor can allow you to demonstrate that the specific question (and the underlying issue it addresses) is not a problem for you. By showing that you are not knocked off balance by the question, you can impress the interviewer more with a lighter answer than if you had tried to answer the question seriously.

Although humor can be risky in an interview and is challenging to apply appropriately, it is often the best tool for dealing with tough questions. For example, if the interviewer asks, "Would you like to sit in my chair one day?" you might respond, "Yes, if you find another chair that's more comfortable!" It is never a good idea, however, to use humor if you have not built up some rapport with your interviewer. Proceed with caution!

11. Be Honest——It's Still the Best Policy

If you think fudging the truth (either by distortion or omission) is no big deal, think again. It's never a good strategy to lie during an interview. The most common lies people tell involve the nature and extent of their education, credentials, or experience, which can be easily checked (and usually are) by a thorough employer. Furthermore, if candidates are hired based on a lie, it will quickly become apparent that they don't possess the background or skills they had claimed. You should know, too, that most lies told in the hiring process rarely turn the tide for interviewers. Many interviewers say the information that most people lie about isn't a critical factor in the decision to hire or not hire them. So when faced with a difficult question, don't try to fool interviewers; they will know that you are avoiding something, and they will keep probing until they get to the bottom of it. You are much better off admitting the truth, stating what you learned, and then moving on to another topic.

Although it's very important to be honest in an interview, you should avoid being *overly* honest—that is, never divulge sensitive or negative information or speak badly of anyone, especially a former supervisor. For instance, do not tell your interviewer that your last boss was terrible or that your coworkers were lazy and expected you to do their work. Do not feel that you must, for honesty's sake, rant on about their shortcomings! By criticizing and dwelling on others' negative traits, you will end up making yourself look bad. If your boss or coworkers were less than stellar, briefly acknowledge that you didn't always see eye-to-eye and then state what you learned from the experience. For example, you might say, "My boss and I often had differences of opinion, but our interactions taught me how to stand up for my point of view in a calm, persuasive manner." By focusing on the positive outcome of an unpleasant situation, you will demonstrate that you can handle challenging coworkers and circumstances.

12. Control Your Body Language

Unfortunately, it's easy to betray your anxiety with nonverbal language, which often happens as an immediate and unconscious response. When faced with a difficult or embarrassing question, some people respond by coughing, blushing, looking down at the floor, playing with their hair, wringing their hands, tapping their foot, and so on. Interviewers easily pick up on these signs—even subtler and less visible ones such as tensing your facial muscles or drooping your shoulders slightly. These unintentional gestures often raise a red flag for interviewers and prompt them to dig deeper.

The only effective way to combat this unconscious behavior is to prepare for questions that make you uncomfortable and practice your responses ahead of time with a friend. Ask him or her to pay close attention to any body language that might reveal your true feelings. You can also practice by looking in a mirror. Practice your responses until you've mastered any bad habits; the more you do this, the better you will become at controlling your nonverbal language.

13. Keep It Professional

Some interviewers have a gift for putting the candidate at ease right away because of their informal and laid-back style. Tread carefully here—these interviewers may make you feel so relaxed that you confess or share things that are better left out of the interview. No matter how nice that interviewer seems (and might, in fact, be), you are not his or her buddy. Keep your guard up and remain professional. Don't cross the line by thinking that you can tell your interviewer your deepest secrets.

14. Smile, Relax, and Look Happy

Few things are more powerful than smiling confidently when sitting face to face with someone who could determine your future. During your interview, make eye contact regularly with your interviewer, and let him or her know that you are relaxed and prepared. You may be scared or even paralyzed inside by a tough question, but what matters is how you look on the outside.

You can master this technique with practice, just as you can fix any body language problems. Look at your smile in the mirror. Avoid a fake expression and be sincere. When you convey the message that there is no question you would rather answer, the interviewer will be impressed.

15. Ask Great Questions Yourself

Many savvy interviewers will tell you that as much as 50 percent of their decision to hire someone is based on the questions that the candidate asks *them*. Candidates who take the time to come up with good, penetrating questions demonstrate their interest in the job, their creativity, and their ability to think on their feet.

Bring a fallback list of ten or so questions for the interviewer, but make sure not to ask any that address information that's already been covered during the interview. Pay attention during the entire interview and ask questions as you go along. You can ask interviewers to elaborate on the job tasks and duties early on so that you can select relevant questions and avoid wasting their time with extraneous inquiries. Ask well thought-out questions that show that you know the company or industry; let them see your enthusiasm and interest in the job. If your interviewer does not ask you essential questions, take the lead and ask what information you can provide to help him or her make a decision.

When you reach the end of the interview and it's your chance to ask questions, don't ask about benefits and salary if you haven't thought of anything else to ask! Instead, reassert your interest in the job and the company.

#1

CONCERN #1:
CAN YOU DO THE JOB?

Do you have sufficient experience, training, education, aptitude, and interest to be productive?

Can you deliver what the organization needs from this position?

How has your background prepared you for this job?

What have you achieved up to now?

What do you know about this job and company?

1 What interests you most about this job?

1 What interests you most about this job?

- I'm most interested in this job because it will allow me to use my enthusiasm, knowledge, and skills.

- This job is a natural continuation of my past X years as a _____ (mention a title or activity).

- The job interests me because of the tasks involved; your company interests me because of its strategy and values.

- This job offers what I am most interested in: a good balance between short- and long-term tasks and projects.

- I love the tasks associated with this job, and I know that I am well qualified to carry them out.

- I would like to fully commit myself to the following three tasks: X, Y, Z (mention tasks from the job description and elaborate on them).

2 What do you think this job will offer you?

2 What do you think this job will offer you?

- A chance to have contact with customers.

- The opportunity to use my favorite skills of _____ (name three).

- The scope of my responsibilities, which I understand to include _____ and _____.

- I have studied your company and know that you are _____ and _____; both of these are very attractive to me.

- This is exactly the job I have wanted for some time. It will offer me the ability to _____ and _____, two of my strongest skills.

- I am a people person, so I find the opportunity to help and interact with others very appealing.

3 **What did you like most and least in your last job?**

3 What did you like most and least in your last job?

- I really liked brainstorming ideas in team meetings.

- What I liked most were the challenges I found there. For example, I particularly liked _____. (Don't mention what you liked least; change the subject.)

- Like most people, I enjoyed routine work the least. What I liked the most, however, was _____ (mention something of value for the job you are pursuing and finish on a positive note).

- The most: creativity. I love to _____.

- The least: the repetitive tasks needed to keep things running smoothly; however, I found that I could make this work more satisfying by accomplishing it as well as possible and finding ways to make the routine more effective and efficient. The most: _____.

- I found it challenging to handle the volume of email that I received, but I knew it was important to respond promptly. It was satisfying to get the inbox whittled down quickly.

4 **How many people have you supervised at any given time?**

4 How many people have you supervised at any given time?

- In my current job, I supervise X employees.

- Between X and Y, depending on the size of the project.

- I have had experience supervising small administrative and production teams.

- I have not had the chance to supervise others yet, but I am fully prepared to do so.

- I often volunteer for community activities and find myself in charge of many people during these projects. The groups range in size from X to Y.

- I was in charge of a group project that involved X people, although I did not have the responsibility of their day-to-day supervision. The project was a great success, and as the project manager, I made sure that we finished ahead of schedule and under budget by $Y.

5 What financial responsibilities have you had?

5 What financial responsibilities have you had?

- I was responsible for a budget of $X at my last job.

- In each of my last three jobs, my level of financial responsibilities has increased. I started the first job with a budget of $X, and my last job had a budget of $Y.

- I have had technical responsibilities that translated into financial responsibilities. As my time in the company progressed, I was not only responsible for the technical aspects of my department but had financial responsibilities for purchasing and implementation.

- I have not yet had financial responsibility in my jobs, but I feel that I can handle this well once I am familiar with all aspects of the job.

- Financially, I haven't yet had direct responsibility, but I have been responsible for managing a team of X people.

- I was in charge of a very important project that meant $X to the company in terms of profit. Though I did not have direct budget responsibilities, my leadership was critical to the success of the project.

- I managed to multiply sales threefold in an eighteen-month period from $X to $Y.

6 **What is the most difficult decision you have had to make in the last twelve months?**

6 What is the most difficult decision you have had to make in the last twelve months?

- (Mention a problem you faced and the decision you made to successfully solve it.)

- I had to determine whether I should fire someone.

- I had to decide whether to stay with my former employer or look for a new job.

- I had to determine whether we should scale back our plans for the expansion of my department.

- As the head of my department, I had to decide whether to reduce my salary and those of my employees in order to prevent personnel cuts.

- I had to decide whether I should accept a promotion and stay with my first employer or return to school to finish my degree. I chose _____ because _____.

7 Which of your achievements has given you the greatest satisfaction?

7 Which of your achievements has given you the greatest satisfaction?

- (Describe something you did professionally that you are proud of and explain why you feel satisfaction about it.)

- I was able to double our productivity and reduce our costs by 40 percent.

- I managed to solve a problem that my coworkers thought would be impossible.

- I was able to complete a project in less time than anticipated and under budget!

- I was honored for (a particular achievement).

- I was able to persevere in the face of a great obstacle and meet my goal of _____.

- (Describe successfully implementing a project similar to the one you would undertake in the position you're seeking.)

- My junior year in college, I received an award for _____. This distinction allowed me to intern with _____, which was a goal I had set for myself.

8 Do you think you are underqualified for this job?

8 Do you think you are underqualified for this job?

- I think I have the potential for the job because _____ (list two or three reasons).

- I am eager to attend an intensive continuing education program to meet the qualifications.

- For some aspects of the job, perhaps. However, I offer your company _____, _____, and _____ (mention three qualities and/or skills).

- Is there a specific skill that concerns you?

- I think I have the skills and enthusiasm necessary for this job.

- Perhaps I can elaborate on my experience or knowledge in the area of _____.

9 Would you be willing to undergo psychological testing?

9 Would you be willing to undergo psychological testing?

- Yes. Could you just let me know how important these tests are in your decision-making process?

- Yes, that would be fine. I am open to any tool that helps to define my job profile.

- Certainly. I would only ask you to share the test results with me, as is customary, I believe.

- Yes, certainly; can you tell me which tests you use?

- I would prefer that you judge me on my professional achievements, and I am ready to answer any questions you have. (Warning: You may alienate the interviewer or raise a red flag if you show reluctance to take a psychological test.)

10 What have you learned from your previous jobs?

10 What have you learned from your previous jobs?

- I have learned how to multitask and manage complex planning where necessary.

- I have learned how to work autonomously and set priorities. For example, _____.

- I have learned that every task I have undertaken is important, even the routine ones. The sum of the parts makes the whole job interesting and exciting.

- I have learned that I enjoy a working environment that is open and honest and allows for give and take from everyone.

- I have learned that I prefer working for a smaller/larger company because _____.

- I have learned how to prioritize the importance of tasks and make sure they are done efficiently and effectively. For instance, _____.

- My jobs have taught me that in spite of situations that are sometimes complicated to manage, there is always something to be learned and a way to grow personally. (Provide an example.)

11 **In your last job, did you discover
a problem that your predecessors
had left untreated?**

11 In your last job, did you discover a problem that your predecessors had left untreated?

- Yes; I discovered a problem that helped me develop a new technique. (Describe it.)

- On my resume, I've mentioned a problem I solved at my last job; it involved _____.

- No. I found my predecessors to have been extremely capable and thorough. I was able to build on the solid foundation they had established.

- No, but I assumed a new responsibility that had not been part of my predecessor's duties. My former boss didn't have time to troubleshoot a particularly difficult project, so he asked me to step in. He was so pleased with my problem-solving skills that he asked me to accept the additional responsibility of _____ from that point on.

- Honestly, I can't say that any particular problem was attributable to my predecessors. To me, it was most important to solve the problems we faced rather than worry about who was responsible for them.

12 What type of job is best suited to you: staff or management?

12 What type of job is best suited to you: staff or management?

- I've found that both roles are often needed in the same job, and doing well at one actually helps me to do well at the other.

- In my last job, I wore a two hats: management and staff. I was adept at and felt comfortable in both.

- I function well in both situations, but I have a preference for _____ (specify which one and explain why).

- I think my greatest skills pertain to a _____ role (mention one) because _____.

- I think I am best suited to a staff job. I am extremely good at following directions and getting the job done.

- I think I am best suited to a management job. I am a natural leader and prefer to take the lead whenever possible.

13 **What do you see as the major trends in our field?**

13 What do you see as the major trends in our field?

- I made a survey in preparation for meeting with you, and I see two main points. (Mention two, such as "cutting costs" or "increasing quality.")

- I see a trend toward _____ that I think has tremendous potential. This is why I want to work in this field.

- From what I know now, I see a slight shift in _____. I'm eager to immerse myself in the reality of the market and study the factors that affect our field.

- I think our field is becoming more technologically advanced, and having skills in this area is a must for the future.

- On the economic side, it looks like we are moving toward _____ because _____.

14 **Why do you think you have the potential for this job?**

14 Why do you think you have the potential for this job?

- I know my potential, and I can tell you that I plan to enrich the company in two areas. (Mention two areas in which you are 100 percent sure you can add value.)

- I can answer that positively for two reasons. (Mention two examples or facts as proof.)

- My three strongest qualifications for this job are _____, _____, and _____.

- Based on the information you have shared with me today, I can say that I have the potential as well as the enthusiasm and persistence that you would expect from someone working for your company.

- I have encountered situations and challenges in my previous jobs that are similar to those involved with this position and I have a successful track record. (Elaborate on one.)

15 Do you think you are overqualified for this job?

15 Do you think you are overqualified for this job?

- Perhaps, but I'm looking to make a long-term commitment in my career now with your company. I hope in time you will see the other ways that I can help this company and in doing so help myself.

- Because of my unusually strong experience in _____, I could start to contribute right away, perhaps much faster than someone who'd have to be brought along more slowly.

- For this job, my previous experience fits well, and I think my qualifications are right for the position; this gives me confidence that I can perform the tasks required in this job.

- Are you concerned about any particular qualification in my resume? I'd be happy to discuss it.

- If I am, you will have the advantage of those extra qualifications and experience to use as needed.

- You could be right, but having had many good jobs in my career has placed me in the fortunate position of being able to do what gives me the greatest satisfaction—and what I enjoy doing most is _____ (describe the job responsibilities).

16 **How would you describe the position for which you are applying?**

16 How would you describe the position for which you are applying?

- In this job, one has to _____ (list the key tasks that are critical for the position).

- This is a difficult job with challenges to meet and demanding customers to satisfy.

- The kind of job that requires _____ and _____ to do well. I have done both these things in my career.

- This is the kind of job I have wanted for some time. I have done quite a bit of research on jobs like this one, and I see that I can match your needs in these major areas: _____ (name three or four).

- I see this job as one focused on _____ (name several key tasks of the position), which require the skills of _____, _____, and _____. I'd be happy to elaborate on how I'd put these skills to work to reach your company's goals.

- I would like to ask you more about the job and return to this question when I have a better understanding of what it involves. Is that okay with you?

17 How do you improve yourself professionally?

17 How do you improve yourself professionally?

- Three ways come to mind: I read professional magazines, attend conferences, and take continuing education courses.

- I keep up with technical breakthroughs and study them to make sure I understand their value for our industry.

- I enjoy trying new things; this helps me develop new skills and interests. For example, _____.

- I am fortunate to have a mentor who is helpful in guiding me on career issues. Together we look for ways I can improve and challenge myself.

- I take one class a semester at my local community college to broaden my knowledge base; right now it's a course in _____.

- I am just starting my career and find that talking with my co-workers about their jobs, skills, and interests helps me gain a "big picture" perspective.

18 **What are your greatest achievements?**

18 What are your greatest achievements?

- (Mention three achievements; for example, launching products X, Y, and Z; reorganizing a division; handling quality control of A, B, and C.) Would you like me to describe one of these in more detail?

- Being a very social person, I always strive to improve relationships among people in the organizations where I've worked.

- I've increased positive results, decreased costs, and avoided errors at every company where I've worked. Can I give you an example of each?

- I was promoted to manager of my company when I was only twenty-three, even though there were many employees older than me. My boss saw my potential and took a risk on me that she said paid off.

- I managed a project that helped change the direction of my team/department/company for the better. (Explain.)

- I have regularly been promoted to positions of greater responsibility throughout my career.

- I graduated from college with distinction and served as a teaching assistant for two professors.

19 How would you describe your ideal working conditions?

19 How would you describe your ideal working conditions?

- (Mention two or three things you need to feel happy in your job that have to do with the people you work with, the physical plant, the location, your values, and the like.)

- I've learned that I do my best work in an environment that is open and light.

- I need to work in a collaborative environment that fosters give and take among the team members.

- I like to work without a lot of daily supervision. I am a self-starter and very motivated once I am given a task to do.

- I prefer to work alone for most of the day so I can concentrate fully on my tasks.

- I am a social person and like the camaraderie of working closely with other people.

- I prefer a work environment that involves a certain amount of pressure to keep the creative juices flowing. I find I am at my best when there is a sense of urgency to my projects.

20 Are you looking for a limited or unlimited time contract?

20 Are you looking for a limited or unlimited time contract?

- What options can you offer?

- A limited-time contract would suit me best because _____.

- A full-time contract would suit me best because _____.

- Before we discuss the details of a contract, I'd like to make sure I'm clear on the responsibilities of the job.

- I am most attracted by an interesting job; the time frame for any contract is of secondary concern.

- I am open to any possibility.

21 **What would you do if you were completely overwhelmed with work and knew you couldn't meet the deadline?**

21 What would you do if you were completely overwhelmed with work and knew you couldn't meet the deadline?

- This has happened to me twice. The first time I handled it by _____; the second time, I _____.

- If I saw that I wouldn't be able to meet the deadline, I would immediately speak to my boss, outline the problems, and see how we might work together to minimize the delay.

- As soon as possible, I would inform the person who set the deadline, and tell him or her what progress I had made and how much more time I would need to finish the project.

- I would ask several people I trust how I might find ways to meet the deadline and see what they suggest.

- I would look for options that might allow some part of the project to be revised so that the majority of it could be completed on time.

- I would ask my boss to prioritize the duties so that the most important ones were done first.

22 Do you prefer to work alone or in a group?

22 Do you prefer to work alone or in a group?

- I can adapt to any situation. I like working on a team because I enjoy the creative energy that flows, but I also like working alone so I can really focus and get things done.

- There are benefits to each. I find that working on my own allows for reflection, whereas working in a group can stimulate ideas and creativity.

- It would seem ideal to me to divide my time between focused hands-on work by myself and a collaborative group exchange.

- I like to split my time 50/50, because many decisions need to be made in group meetings but the actual work of getting the job done can be handled independently.

- I'm used to spending most of my work time working alone, but I would like to change the balance to more time spent as part of a team.

- I'm used to spending most of my work time working on a team; now I would like to change the balance so I have more time to work independently.

23 How do you learn best?

23 How do you learn best?

- I learn best by doing.

- I have several different learning techniques that work well for me. In situations like _____, I learn best by _____; in a situation like _____, I learn best by _____.

- I observe, I listen, I read, and then I put into practice what I've learned. That's what works for me.

- I always plan my schedule so I can concentrate on my studies as much as on my work. I like to read everything I can find about a subject.

- My learning technique involves a combination of creativity, logic, and memorization.

- I like to read manuals and then try it out for myself. I find if I have clear instructions, I can do most things.

24 Do you think job security exists anymore?

24 Do you think job security exists anymore?

- Not really. The marketplace is changing so fast now that it's hard to imagine many jobs where real security still exists.

- It's still possible, but it takes effort. The best way to try to gain job security is to do your job well and continually strive for more responsibilities. The best way to keep your job is to love the job you do.

- Some jobs seem more stable and less prone to turnover, like those that offer tenure, while others are riskier, such as those in the ever-changing new technologies sector.

- I don't think about job security very much. I am far more concerned with making sure the job I have is fulfilling and provides my employer with the skills and results they need from me.

- As the global market continues to grow, what we once thought of as job security has dwindled. The up side to this is that with technological advances, new jobs are being created all the time, so with uncertainty there's also opportunity.

- When the economy slows and unemployment rises, it is harder to keep a job. During difficult times, workers must be more flexible and prove the value they can deliver to their current employer—or a new employer.

25 I have three candidates, including you, for this position. What criteria should I use to decide who to hire?

25 I have three candidates, including you, for this position. What criteria should I use to decide who to hire?

- I would love this job. I hope that I have demonstrated to you that I possess the necessary skills and experience to do it well. That said, I think you should pick me!

- You should choose the person you think has the needed skills and the strongest track record. You mentioned three areas that are most important to you, and I believe I meet all three of those needs: _____, _____, and _____.

- Could you tell me what you have found most valuable in the two other candidates? (If possible, describe how you also possess these skills/qualities, then list several of your other strong attributes; if the employer cites criteria you don't share, point out what you can offer that would make up for these.)

- You should consider whether I have the skills that you need, whether I share your company's values and goals, and whether I will fit in well at your organization. Have I provided this information to your satisfaction?

- If your three criteria are competency, enthusiasm, and perseverance, then I am the person for the job.

- Above all, authenticity and honesty.

- A steady, grounded personality and good self-management skills are essential for this position.

26 How much time will you need on the job before you are fully productive?

26 How much time will you need on the job before you are fully productive?

- Very little. I believe I have a good understanding of the tasks and responsibilities; once I've had a chance to meet my co-workers, get oriented, and settle in, I will be fully productive in this position.

- Before I can answer, I would like to ask you two questions. First, what is your top priority for this job? Second, what projects would I need to immediately take responsibility for?

- The time needed to thoroughly study the files for the projects.

- I usually adapt myself fairly quickly; a good estimate would be X to Y weeks.

- I'd expect to start my daily, routine work immediately. For more specific issues, I'd need enough time to learn more about the projects, your company, and your customers.

27 **How does an employer demonstrate social responsibility? Does this matter to you?**

27 How does an employer demonstrate social responsibility? Does this matter to you?

- Businesses need to care about more than just the bottom line. Employers should place value on how their business relates to the larger issues we face as a global community.

- I want to work for a "green" company. It's important to me that my employer cares about the environment and does what it can to stop global warming.

- Employers can demonstrate social responsibility by conducting their business in an ethical way, taking into account their impact on society and the environment.

- Every business, no matter how small or large, can do something to help solve the problems we face today. It may be as simple as replacing Styrofoam cups with paper cups, or as complicated as providing vans for carpooling.

- I want to work for an employer who respects the rights of human beings at local, national, and global levels and is not just interested in those who buy its products. I think businesses that demonstrate social responsibility will have employees who are more satisfied with their jobs, share similar values, and become more committed to achieving success.

- It is not of primary importance to me. I want to work for an employer whose first priority is maintaining the well-being of its own employees.

#2

CONCERN #2:
WHO ARE YOU?

What do you like and dislike?

What are your main characteristics and traits?

What is your personality like?

What are your values and goals?

28 So?

28 So?

This question is often asked as the interview is getting started, after introductions have been made. The interviewer may be testing how you respond to an ambiguous question and whether you are eager to take the initiative.

- May I be seated?

- Thank you for taking the time to meet with me this afternoon. I'm looking forward to our discussion.

- Where would you like to begin?

- Would you like me to talk about myself or would you rather give me some details about the job?

- I have approached you because _____ (briefly state the reason). I am hoping that you can tell me some more details about your organization.

- Thank you for the interview. May we start by clarifying two tasks in the job description? (Name them.)

- Before we begin, may I ask you what it was in my letter and resume that made you decide to invite me for an interview?

29 Tell me about yourself.

29 **Tell me about yourself.**

This is a very general inquiry, so feel free to ask a follow-up question to get a better idea of what the interviewer wants, then develop your response in less than two minutes.

- Certainly. What specific area would you like me to discuss: my work experience or work style?

- With pleasure! Would you like me to discuss a past achievement or a recent one? (When the interviewer states a preference, respond with an example.)

- Should I develop something in detail or just give you a brief summary? (When the interviewer states a preference, respond with a one-minute overview of your experience or an accomplishment that exemplifies your personal strengths.)

- In my career I've pursued two paths, both of which are relevant to your company's activities. (Elaborate on them.)

- Here are three things I've accomplished during my career so far, which I believe illustrate what kind of person I am: _____, _____, and _____.

- I am a person who loves to _____, and I demonstrate that by _____ (use only a work-related example).

- Three of my personal traits fit particularly well with the job you are offering: my _____, _____, and _____.

30 What makes you unique?

30 What makes you unique?

- Three things: my _____, _____, and _____ (list three skills or personal characteristics that relate to the job).

- I have a unique combination of strengths for a prospective employer: a sound basic technical background, additional training in management, and international experience.

- Several employers have told me they particularly value my contributions because I pay attention to detail, am never late, and know how to find needed information at a moment's notice.

- I take a different approach from most people: I _____ (give one or two examples).

- I have the skills, enthusiasm, and knowledge to excel at the tasks required for this job. In my experience in this field, it's hard to find a candidate with all three qualifications.

- I have a natural gift for relating well to people, and I am a very good listener. In my work in this industry, I've found that many employees have strong technical skills and great energy and dedication, yet they often have trouble communicating in a real give-and-take style that supports collaboration.

- I think it's my combination of skills and personality that makes me unique. I am a good _____, I dream big, and I can be counted on to follow through.

31 How do you respond when your ideas are rejected?

31 How do you respond when your ideas are rejected?

- I take a few minutes to regroup and then find out why my proposal was rejected. Once I understand the reason, I work to fix any problems, then take another run at the solution.

- I do not give up, but remain persistent in finding a solution that wins approval.

- I once had an idea that was rejected at first, but later it was accepted and with slight modifications it turned out to be a great success. (Explain the situation in greater detail.)

- Realistically, any employee should expect this to happen periodically. I've always sought out a work environment that is open to the exchange of ideas, even if some are not successful in the end. How would you say your company encourages ideas from its employees?

- I don't mind if my ideas are rejected occasionally. Not every idea can be great. I think it's the willingness to persevere and see things in new ways that keeps an employee engaged.

- I use the opportunity to reexamine my thought process. Perhaps there were factors that I should have considered more carefully or details that I initially overlooked.

- I will advocate for my idea when I feel strongly that it has significant merit or corresponds to a value that is important to the company.

32 What kinds of things cause you to lose interest in a project?

32 What kinds of things cause you to lose interest in a project?

- Like most people, I can lose interest when I have to do the same thing over and over again without any variation in the tasks. I find it's helpful to have several different responsibilities so I can shift focus and stay engaged.

- At times I've found it hard to maintain interest when team members are rigid or cynical; for example, insisting there is only one right way to do things, or trying to deflate other team members' enthusiasm.

- Not having enough work to do and feeling that my talents aren't being used to their fullest. When this happens, I am eager to _____.

- A negative environment in which only problems are discussed. I find it far more stimulating and rewarding when an employer acknowledges and applauds its employees' efforts and accomplishments.

- When there is no expectation that any new responsibilities will be added to my duties. I strive to continually expand my skill base so I can take on more challenges.

33 What do you like to do when you are not working?

33 What do you like to do when you are not working?

Mention athletic or cultural activities you enjoy. However, if you participate in an extracurricular activity that might be seen negatively by the employer or interviewer, do not discuss it.

- I pursue activities different from my work. (For example, "I make pottery, I listen to music," and so on.)

- I use my leisure time to exercise so that I can maintain my energy and stamina. I particularly like _____ (biking, hiking, running, swimming, and the like).

- I play on a softball team with friends from my _____ (school, community, former job).

- I volunteer at the local food bank, filling grocery bags for those without resources.

- I like watching movies and reading nonfiction historical books. (Mention a few favorites—and what you liked about them— that reveal something specific and positive about you.)

- I train and enrich my mind by attending conferences whenever I get the chance. (Mention a few favorites and briefly explain why they were valuable experiences.)

- I love to _____ (name something you enjoy that is related to some aspect of this job or company; for instance, if you work in the auto industry, you might say "I love to attend car shows").

34 **How do you react when you realize that you have made a mistake?**

34 How do you react when you realize that you have made a mistake?

- I take time to analyze the situation carefully and then take corrective steps.

- I apologize to those involved and work harder to make sure it doesn't happen again.

- I look to see what caused me to make the mistake so I can prevent it from happening again.

- It's my experience that everyone makes mistakes occasionally. When it happens to me, I acknowledge my share of responsibility and get back to work again.

- I reflect on what happened and talk with friends and coworkers about what I could do differently next time.

- I discuss the situation with my supervisor and develop a strategy so I don't repeat my mistake. The upside of mistakes is that we get to learn from them to become better employees.

35 *Silence.*

35 *Silence.*

This is one tactic that interviewers use to test your response to stress. Refuse to be intimidated, and do not feel compelled to start talking because you are nervous about a little silence! Speak only if you really have something to say.

- (Count to eight on your fingers under the table. Usually the interviewer will resume talking before you reach eight.)

- (Ask a question that changes the subject to something your interviewer seemed interested in discussing.)

- (Ask a question about the company or department.)

- (Ask for additional information on a particular task or responsibility of the job.)

- Do you have any other questions for me that will help you determine whether I am the right person for this job?

- If we have covered everything, which of us will initiate the next contact? I'm very interested in moving forward to the next stage of the interviewing process.

36 How do you react when you are angry?

36 How do you react when you are angry?

- It bothers me when I am not included in a project for which I think I have the necessary ability or knowledge. Rather than just let my anger build, I will seek out the person who made the decision so I can calmly make my case.

- I am an even-tempered and positive person by nature, and this helps me remain calm, even when I think things are not running smoothly. Communication is the key to keeping things on track and preventing situations that cause anger and upset.

- I back away from the issue for a period of time and collect my thoughts. I do not like reacting too quickly; I find that's usually when people say things they don't mean.

- I speak my mind in a nonthreatening way; I do not believe in pretending nothing is wrong and silently punishing those who have made me upset.

- I can get angry with people whose passivity and lack of effort impede the company's success or progress, so before it reaches that point I always try to use my enthusiasm and energy to inspire and motivate others.

- I remove myself from the situation and write down what is really bothering me. I can usually get to the bottom of issues when I write down my feelings, and I often find that what I am feeling is not so much anger as hurt.

37 How do you operate under stress?

37 How do you operate under stress?

- It stimulates me and makes me more efficient. I am a person who can easily rise to the occasion and focus my energy on the task at hand so it is completed on time.

- Generally, I am well organized and can handle unpredictable setbacks, so I manage to eliminate most causes of stress. If it's unavoidable, I don't let it overwhelm or distract me.

- I work well under pressure. In my last job, I faced a very short deadline for a major project and was able to finish it on time with excellent results.

- I handle stress well. For example, _____ (give a brief example of when you were under stress at work and how you managed the situation).

- Deadlines that come up without a lot of notice are actually exciting to me. I get a lot of satisfaction from meeting that kind of challenge and not letting it get the best of me.

- If the stress is caused by conflict among people, I work hard to resolve it—I've seen how company morale can suffer when disagreements and misunderstandings arise among colleagues, and people tell me I'm an effective mediator.

- When I'm under a lot of stress, I double my efforts to eat well, exercise, and get enough sleep. Maintaining my physical well-being gives me the energy and stamina to face challenging situations at work.

38 What regrets do you have about your career?

38 What regrets do you have about your career?

- I wish I had looked for a job that _____ (mention your career objectives) sooner.

- Honestly, I don't have regrets. I have been very directed about what I want to do; I think that's part of the reason I've always achieved what I wanted most.

- I have always believed in concentrating on the positive side of my professional experiences, so I don't have regrets.

- I am new to the workforce, so I don't really have enough experience yet to have any regrets.

- I regret not applying myself earlier in my career when I thought it wouldn't matter if I moved around a bit. As I've matured, I have come to understand that doing what you really love is what matters most in a career.

- I regret not being able to use all of my creative potential in some of my past jobs.

39 Don't you trust that we will follow through with this agreement?

39 Don't you trust that we will follow through with this agreement?

This question is usually raised if you request a written commitment after you are given a verbal promise.

- I only wish to formalize the agreement we have just made. This way we can ensure there will be no problems in communication.

- Yes, of course. I am only suggesting that we summarize, in writing, the key information so there can be no misunderstandings down the road.

- Yes, but it's likely that others in the company—such as my future supervisor or human resources personnel—will need to know the details of our agreement. This way we can be sure to cover all the points of our agreement so everyone is on the same page.

- Yes, I do. However, it would be helpful to me to have our agreement in writing so I can take time to look through it carefully.

- My request for a written agreement has nothing to do with trust. I believe it is best for professionals to write things down whenever possible to prevent needless problems from arising in the future.

40 What are your strengths and weaknesses?

40 What are your strengths and weaknesses?

- (Mention three strengths, two minor weaknesses, one strength; then change the subject.)

- I think it will be most helpful for your decision making to know my three key characteristics (mention three strengths).

- May I tell you about two achievements that reveal a lot about my character?

- I am enthusiastic, energetic, and willing to work hard. Some coworkers have told me that at first they thought I was aloof or unfriendly—but once they got to know me, they realized I was just very focused on what I was doing. Knowing this, I try to slow down and make an extra effort to connect with people.

- I am a very focused person, so sometimes it is hard for me to switch gears. For example, I tend to work for long stretches at the computer without a break. I find it really helpful to schedule break reminders with a software program I have, which allows me to take some time to feel refreshed and recharged.

- I am dedicated to finishing the tasks I undertake and making sure no detail is overlooked. Even though I'm new to the job market, I'm confident that these strengths will carry over into my responsibilities for this position and help me develop more specific skills.

41 What do you most want to improve in the next year?

41 What do you most want to improve in the next year?

- I'd like to improve my own performance, which should help my subordinates to boost their performance too.

- I'd like to become better at anticipating the needs of the market for _____ (name the product or service).

- On the work front, I would like to take a class on _____ to improve my skills for _____. On a purely personal note, my swing and my handicap. Do you play golf? (This is effective if you've confirmed that golf is a popular component of this company's business-related extracurricular activities. Substitute skiing, tennis, marathons—any activity that you genuinely participate in and know is enjoyed by your potential colleagues here.)

- Are you speaking in terms of my transferable skills, knowledge, or personality traits? (Give an example for the one the interviewer indicates.)

- The two concerns about your organization that you mentioned (increasing your market share, retaining your key customers, and so on).

- I am very interested in learning _____ (a new computer program, management technique or technology, or some cutting-edge skills relevant to your profession).

42 **Can you give me some examples of your creativity on the job?**

42 Can you give me some examples of your creativity on the job?

- I planned, organized, and put on a trade show last year that was a big success. I had to be very creative in my design and implementation for the booth.

- I am very analytical and can look at an issue from all sides, appreciating the mind-set of those with different viewpoints.

- I am a good manager who listens to my team members; I work hard to figure out and give them what they need to perform their jobs well.

- In my last/present job, I _____ and _____ (mention two achievements highlighting your creativity).

- I think creativity is the ability to look at something in a new and different way and find new possibilities. I do that by _____.

- I think about things and then figure out how to turn my thoughts into reality. It's not enough to just be imaginative; creativity also means acting on your thoughts and ideas.

43 How would you describe your personality?

43 How would you describe your personality?

Pause for a moment to think, so you don't seem overrehearsed. Consider your *real* personality and not what you think the interviewer wants to hear.

- (Mention two or three of your key traits that apply to the job.)

- I find that challenges and problems stimulate me rather than frighten me.

- I am a worker bee! I do whatever it takes to get the job done.

- I am a fast learner. I can hit the ground running after a short period of time.

- I am an analyzer! I love to study data and dig out the useful information.

- I am reliable and pride myself on getting the job done, done right, and done on time!

- I am a people person—I get energized by my interactions with others. By nature I am an extrovert; I thrive on building relationships with those around me.

44 How do you react when you are told your methodology isn't working?

44 How do you react when you are told your methodology isn't working?

- I listen to the reasons and see if there is merit in the feedback before I change my strategy.

- I am usually very adaptable, and I like to receive honest input from others.

- Initially, it can be hard to hear that my methods aren't working, but in fact, it's often stimulating to look at things in new ways, so I seize the opportunity to improve my skills.

- I am open to new and different ways to accomplish my tasks, and I am willing to negotiate a new time frame and approach to carry out the tasks.

- I ask how and why it isn't working; if there is a different technique that leads to a better outcome, I accept it.

45 How do you define success?

45 How do you define success?

- I think success has to be proven by measurable results. For example, due to my determination that my team members receive excellent training, we lowered the turnover rate by 8 percent in six months, despite serious competition.

- I see success as constantly moving toward the goals I have set for myself and living up to my commitments.

- Success is a journey, and it changes over time. For me now, it's living up to my potential and having a job in which I can really make a positive difference.

- I define success as having a positive attitude. I believe positive things happen to positive people.

- Success is the ability to keep learning things and letting this knowledge enrich my life and relationships. I don't see success as reaching an end point; I never want to feel I know all there is to know.

- Success is persevering in the face of obstacles. Not giving up, no matter what problems arise.

- To me, success is reaching one's goals with honesty and integrity. There are plenty of people who have succeeded by abandoning these principles, but they often pay a price at some point down the road.

46 What is your leadership style?

46 What is your leadership style?

- I instill enthusiasm into my team and use my energy and dedication to move my team forward.

- I like to involve others in the decision-making process; if we succeed, the credit is shared by all, but if things don't turn out as we planned, I will take responsibility for whatever decision was made.

- I like to lead by example. I believe that my values and ideals will inspire others to follow me.

- I like doing things by the book, especially when the safety of my employees is at stake.

- I don't like to interfere too much with the work of my employees. I trust them to do their jobs well and I know they don't need someone looking over their shoulders 24-7. But when they need guidance or advice, I'm always there for them.

- My leadership style is participative and interactive; I like to support and actively mentor those on my team.

- I believe in getting the job done. I value structure, planning, organization, and a good quality assurance process.

- I am a motivational leader; I like to inspire my team with a shared vision of the future. I'm also approachable; I think it's critical to be visible and accessible to my team, so I make sure to communicate regularly with them and invite their input.

47 What is your favorite website and why?

47 What is your favorite website and why?

When naming a favorite website, choose one that either has an intellectual or educational component or is related to your job or field.

- I like _____ (mention an interesting or unique website) because _____ (provide a compelling and convincing reason).

- I really like howstuffworks.com because it has interesting and interactive information about current news topics and other compelling subjects. Recently, they had information about _____ (provide an example of a recent topic on the website that you enjoyed learning about).

- For shopping, I like Amazon.com because I can always find good books and all kinds of other things for reasonable prices.

- I love websites on _____ (mention a subject related to your job or field), such as _____ (name one or two of your favorite sites).

- I check the *Grandiloquent Dictionary* daily, because it contains some really obscure English words, and it's fun to learn something new every day. Some of my recent favorite entries were _____ (name two words that you found especially memorable and be prepared to define them!).

48 Who has been the biggest source of inspiration in your professional life, and why?

48 Who has been the biggest source of inspiration in your professional life, and why?

- My first boss, because I saw how a good boss can enrich the lives of his employees. Today, I put into practice what I learned from him: always treating people with respect and appreciation.

- My father, because he taught me that there is dignity in every job. He started his career in the mailroom and worked his way up by believing that everyone and every job has value.

- My mentor, because she continually supports me and urges me to try new things and risk failure in order to find success. I hope to one day mentor someone else as well as she has mentored me.

- A teacher I had in the sixth grade; she saw uniqueness and excellence in every student and made each of us feel special. A gift like that is rare, and I have followed her example in my professional life by striving to make personal connections with those around me.

- _____, who excelled at his job and made me realize that greatness is something you earn over time by following through on your commitments and living up to the high standards you set.

- I am inspired by others who excel at what they do, yet have overcome tremendous obstacles in order to find happiness. For instance, _____ (name a person and explain why he or she fits this description).

49 What is your work style?

49 **What is your work style?**

- I am a collaborative worker. I value the contributions of others and work hard to build team spirit and a feeling of value for every member of my team/department.

- I am a go-getter. I like to get right into the middle of things and solve problems quickly. I love to take on new responsibilities and challenges.

- I am very methodical and organized; I like to make sure that no detail is overlooked.

- I love to work on projects, as they have a beginning, middle, and end. I feel a great sense of accomplishment when I am able to bring a project successfully to completion.

- I am fairly independent and don't need a lot of supervision once I have been assigned a task. I am a self-starter with a lot of internal motivation.

- I am highly goal oriented. I believe in setting goals and working to meet them. For example, at my last job, I undertook _____.

50 What are your future ambitions?

50 What are your future ambitions?

- I'm interested in broadening my skill/knowledge base and learning _____.

- My ambition is to _____ (mention a relevant professional goal), and this job offers me an ideal opportunity to achieve that goal by accomplishing _____ for your company.

- I would like to work in/as _____ (name a department or role that interests you and explain why you find it appealing).

- I plan to learn _____ (name a language that would be advantageous in working for this company) this year.

- I would like to work for a company that allows me to take on more responsibility in the area of _____ so that I could move into a management role within the next three to four years.

51 **What do you think of my style of interviewing? If you were conducting this interview, would you do something differently?**

51 What do you think of my style of interviewing? If you were conducting this interview, would you do something differently?

- I think you have asked good questions to find the right candidate. I hope you decide that I'm that person. (Smile warmly and confidently.)

- I appreciate the way you _____ (mention whatever has been helpful to you; for example, the interviewer pointed out that your professional background was similar to her own or described recent changes at the company); you know this process can be stressful, and you helped make it a little less so.

- I think you have been direct and thorough—the two most important qualities needed to conduct a good interview and get the information you need.

- I think you have done well. You have been very methodical and analytical, and I'm sure that approach will result in selecting the right person for the job.

- You have been very informative and very friendly. I was a bit nervous at first but you helped put me at ease and offered the information I needed to make sure I would be a good fit, which I believe is the case. So, I thank you for that!

- I appreciate that you gave me enough time to thoroughly answer your questions and never made me feel rushed.

52 How did you overcome the negative impact of losing a job?

52 How did you overcome the negative impact of losing a job?

- It was difficult at first, but I persevered by engaging in job hunting activities every day to help overcome my feelings of loss, and now I have recovered.

- At first I felt devastated, but as time went on I saw that it was actually for the best—it opened the door to my finding an even better job.

- I've used the time to further my knowledge in the field of _____. By educating myself, I was able to maintain a sense of focus and keep my confidence intact.

- I followed a very strict routine and schedule so I wouldn't feel so displaced. I work hard every day to reach my goal of finding the right job.

- I took a week off to regroup and spend time with family and friends. Then I got busy contacting my network to let people know I was looking for a new career opportunity. (If you got a lead for this job, mention the person who referred you.)

53 What is your biggest failure and what did you learn from it?

53 What is your biggest failure and what did you learn from it?

Limit your description of the failure to the relevant facts, and don't go into detail about your emotions; devote more time to explaining what you learned from the experience.

- I believe in always having a Plan B for anything I undertake, so if Plan A doesn't succeed, I am prepared to try a second approach. (Describe an unsuccessful "Plan A" and explain what you learned from its failure.)

- Your question comes a little early in my career, but I can relate something from my school days. I once didn't finish a paper on time and was given a poor grade. I learned from that experience that you have to meet deadlines or there will be consequences. Since then, I've never failed to meet a deadline.

- I don't think there is any dishonor in failure unless you fail to learn from it. If you've never failed, it means you've never taken a risk. I learned this lesson when _____ (describe a professional risk that you took that didn't pay off).

- I needed to hire many people when I worked in a fast-growing industry; when the market suffered a downturn, we had to let some of them go. I felt very bad and learned that you have to take a long-range view and not make hasty decisions.

- Early in my career I took a job with a company that I had not thoroughly investigated. I soon found out the company did not play by fair rules, and I left the job. Since then, I always carefully research anything that is important to me.

54 What are your weaknesses and your limitations?

54 What are your weaknesses and your limitations?

Mention things that are not critical to the job and discuss how you are overcoming the problem. Be honest; do not make up something you think the interviewer wants to hear.

- I have difficulty saying no when it's clear I am needed. I find it helpful to keep a wall calendar with my current commitments and deadlines, so I can quickly assess my availability and explain my reasons when I have to decline.

- I feel very passionate about not wasting time, which can occasionally cause me to become impatient with others. To combat this, I remind myself that taking a little extra time to explain the guidelines or expectations for a project often prevents problems down the road.

- When I get overwhelmed, I tend to let my normal organizational tools slip. However, I've been working hard on this problem by taking fifteen minutes at the end of each day to update my calendar, put files in their places, and write a list of priorities for the next day.

- I tend to work too late at night, which can leave me tired the next day. I have recently established a fixed time to go to bed so I can start the day refreshed and energetic.

- Sometimes I have trouble sharing my ideas in front of a large group of people. Recently I've been meeting with my supervisor every week to discuss my thoughts and I've found that her confidence in my ideas has encouraged me to speak up more.

55 Describe your ideal job and employer.

55 Describe your ideal job and employer.

- My ideal job is one in which I can learn, grow, and build my strengths; my ideal employer is one who values employees' contributions and offers opportunities for advancement.

- My ideal job is one that incorporates both my education and practical work skills and allows me to demonstrate my range of abilities. My ideal employer is a mid-size company where people know each other's names.

- My ideal job is in the field of _____, using my skills in _____. I like the idea of a smaller/larger company because _____.

- I want to work as a _____ within the next four to five years. My ideal company would be one that offered the potential of moving into positions of more responsibility.

- My ideal job would offer a lot of creative freedom to try out new ideas. I would love to be part of a company that evolves from a smaller start-up into a bigger business and to participate in its growth and progress.

- (Mention why you are interested in a particular field, then discuss how the job/company would be a fulfilling match. For instance, "My ideal job is in the travel industry. I traveled extensively when I was younger and have always valued learning about different cultures. I would like to work for a travel magazine, which would allow me to combine my love of travel with my skills as a photographer.")

56 What are your long-term professional goals?

56 What are your long-term professional goals?

- I would like to be in a position where I can maximize profitability for the company by investigating potential new areas of business. In my last job, I discovered two untapped markets and successfully incorporated them into our overall strategy. (Explain briefly.)

- (Mention several goals that span a significant time period, which will show the interviewer that you've thought carefully about the progress of your career. For instance, "In five years, I would like to _____. In fifteen years, I hope to _____.")

- To work where I am efficient and can thrive and develop the skills I most like using (name three). In this job, those abilities would benefit your company by _____.

- To work at a job that brings me joy and makes a positive difference to others. I see myself helping people by _____.

- To move into a management position and play a larger role in running the company.

- I would like to return to school in the future to pursue a degree in _____. A strong education is necessary for moving forward in this industry, and I am committed to learning techniques and strategies that will allow me to become a leader.

57 **How would you respond if I told you that your performance today has not been very good?**

57 How would you respond if I told you that your performance today has not been very good?

Do not become defensive or overly apologetic when responding to the interviewer; remain positive, confident, and receptive to any suggestions or constructive criticism. It's often helpful to ask a follow-up question for clarification.

- Did you identify a weakness in my attitude or in the way I express myself?

- May I ask you to elaborate on the areas that I need to improve so I could learn from this experience?

- I'm grateful for the feedback, and if you can give me some specific observations, it would help me focus on where I need to improve. I'm still very interested in this job.

- I think I am the right candidate for this job, and I am a little nervous. I suspect my desire to get the job is so strong that I am overly anxious, so haven't done as well as I hoped.

- I'm hoping that you are asking this as a test to see how I will react! If you are serious, could you tell me what about my performance disappointed you? I'm a bit surprised.

58 What type of decision is the most difficult for you to make?

58 What type of decision is the most difficult for you to make?

- It is difficult for a manager to make unpopular but necessary decisions. However, I know that by communicating openly and honestly about planned changes, I can help everyone involved feel less anxious.

- Firing someone—it never gets easy. It takes compassion and diplomacy.

- When filling a job opening, it's hard to have to choose between two people who are both enthusiastic and competent.

- I do not like to say no when coworkers ask for help; unfortunately though, sometimes it's necessary when I have a lot of work myself and need to be as efficient as possible.

- It can be difficult to choose who gets the best assignments when exciting projects come up. I believe in rewarding those who have done good work, but I also believe that those with less experience need to be given opportunities to prove themselves; otherwise, they may never grow into their potential.

- There have been a few times when I truly believed in a particular project or idea, but my team disagreed. It was difficult for me to decide whether I should stand up for my opinion or defer to the team's decision.

59 Could you describe your worst day and how you dealt with it?

59 Could you describe your worst day and how you dealt with it?

- When my department was cut in half during a major down-sizing, it was very difficult to stay positive, even for those of us who were not let go. I dealt with it by working even harder, to keep my mind off of losing my colleagues.

- My worst day was when my boss told me she was leaving. I really enjoyed working for her and knew I would miss her greatly. When the new boss arrived, I tried to build a strong relationship with her too, even though she was quite different from my former boss.

- I once made a miscalculation for a project, which forced the team to regroup and fix the error. Fortunately, it didn't affect the final outcome of the project, but it did cause extra work for several people. I learned to double-check all my work and review it with others if I have any doubts.

- My worst day was when someone in the company spread gos-sip about me and others on my team. It wasn't true, but it was still hurtful. I spoke with the person who had started the rumor to let him know how his actions had affected us. We managed to smooth things over, and it never happened again.

- My worst day was when I realized that I would not be able to finish all of my projects on time because of unforeseen set-backs. I was disappointed that I had not factored in possible delays and planned accordingly. Now I always build in extra time just in case any unexpected problems occur.

60 Are your past actions consistent with your values?

60 Are your past actions consistent with your values?

- Yes, my beliefs guide my behavior. For example, I value _____ in others, so I emulate that myself by _____.

- I value hard work and commitment. My track record shows that I give 110 percent to any task I undertake, and I always see it through to completion.

- I value working on projects that demand intellect and creativity, so I am always looking for new ways to challenge myself mentally. For example, _____.

- I value good health and lifestyle habits, so I eat right and exercise. I do not like to miss work because I am sick.

- Yes. I value integrity, honesty, and forthrightness, and my behavior reflects this. I would never cheat or lie to my employer or ask others to do what I am not willing to do myself.

61 What will bring you the most satisfaction in your next job?

61 What will bring you the most satisfaction in your next job?

- I would like to fully commit myself to the following three tasks: _____, _____, and _____ (mention tasks in the job description and elaborate on them).

- To become responsible for _____ (name several tasks or duties that you would like to undertake, including at least one that is challenging or innovative).

- I will find great satisfaction by working in a cooperative, team-driven environment where I can also take individual initiative.

- To use my creative talent and problem-solving abilities to _____ and _____.

- I will find satisfaction in my next job if I am given the kind of challenges you've described here today. Specifically, I hope to _____.

- I find satisfaction in knowing I can contribute to the greater good of the world through whatever work I do. I believe in the "think globally, act locally" philosophy; if I help to improve things for people nearby, that example can have a ripple effect.

#3

CONCERN #3:
WILL YOU FIT IN AT THE COMPANY?

Will you be part of a problem or part of a solution?

How do you relate to others?

How have you gotten along with others in your past?

What do you expect from us?

How interested are you in working here?

62 How long will you stay with us?

62 How long will you stay with us?

- I am looking for a long-term position, at least X to Y years.

- As long as I can contribute to the company's development and the relationship is mutually satisfying.

- I am a very loyal person who likes to stay put once I have found a home.

- I like the stability of the company and the variety of tasks and responsibilities this job involves, so I can see myself here for quite some time.

- I am a stable person. I like to follow through with the commitments I have made.

- I see no limit, as long as I feel that I am developing in the position and advancing when I'm ready, and as long as you are pleased with my performance.

63 How would you describe your last boss?

63 How would you describe your last boss?

Never speak negatively about a former boss. If you did not have a good relationship, discuss the positive things you learned from him or her.

- A knowledgeable, accomplished specialist in the field.

- She is a very competent person who excels at her job and inspires confidence.

- A person who has excellent relationships with his subordinates and people in general.

- Due to the nature of my job, we had limited contact. Our relationship was satisfactory but not overly personal.

- I learned a lot from him; specifically, _____ (mention two or three important lessons your boss taught you—for instance, how to interact with others in the workplace, how to negotiate successfully, how to defend what you believe in, and so on).

- Our relationship was good and I enjoyed working with her. We had many lively and productive discussions.

- My last boss was terrific. We had clear lines of communication and each of us knew what to expect from the other. There was a high level of trust between us.

- Excellent. She said she would be happy to be contacted for a reference. Would you like her contact information?

64 **How do you contribute to team spirit?**

64 How do you contribute to team spirit?

- I love collaborating with a group when working on a project—it helps strengthen interpersonal bonds and cultivates a sense of cooperation. I'm eager to contribute to building that kind of solidarity at my next job.

- I love to work as part of a team because I appreciate all the different skills and viewpoints that everyone contributes. I boost team spirit by promoting an open exchange of ideas and encouraging people to use their various talents and abilities.

- I enjoy hearing my colleagues' thoughts and sharing my own ideas; I've also found that my talent for implementing ideas often contributes to the team's overall progress. This approach really boosts morale and trust within the team.

- I'm a true team player and try to ensure that each person's opinions are heard and respected, which creates a feeling of equality. When *everyone* feels that his or her thoughts are valued, the overall team spirit really thrives.

- I value collegiality and the give-and-take that happens when people work side-by-side to meet the same goals. I thrive when called on to take the lead; as a leader, I try to strengthen team spirit by praising the group's progress, encouraging compromise, and promoting constructive communication.

65 Why were you let go from your last job?

65 Why were you let go from your last job?

- My division was relocated, and I wanted to stay in this area.

- My employer was not able to offer me a position matching my professional objectives.

- The project for which I was responsible was completed. I saw it through to the end, but realized that with only a limited number of openings in the regular staff, I would be better off looking for another job. I see this as an opportunity, not a loss.

- My division was completely eliminated for strategic and budgetary reasons beyond my control.

- My employer wanted to steer me into a position in which my skills would not have been used profitably. I told him that I didn't want to pursue that opportunity and we agreed that it would be wise for me to seek a company that was a better fit.

- I was not following through with all of my duties. I took responsibility for this, and my boss can vouch for the fact that I am much improved. But in the process, I realized that the job was very isolated, and that I perform best as a member of a collaborative team, like the position you are offering.

- My supervisor and I tried our best to work out our disagreements over _____, but we never found common ground, so it was in everyone's best interest for me to leave.

66 How do you think your subordinates perceive you?

66 How do you think your subordinates perceive you?

- They would say I am organized and detail oriented.

- They see me as someone who has high expectations, but is fair and open to discussion.

- They consider me approachable and amenable to constructive suggestions. I am easy to get along with, and I've been told I'm a good mediator.

- When I joined the company, morale in the department was low and turnover was high. In the two years I've been there, turnover has decreased significantly. I can't take sole credit for this, but I did work hard to _____ (give some examples of how you tried to increase retention), and one person told me that the improvement had changed her mind about leaving.

- They see me as a hard worker; they know I would not ask them to do anything that I am not willing to do myself.

- They consider me an adviser and supporter; they feel comfortable coming to me with their problems. I believe in helping others grow and mature in their jobs.

67 **Describe the most difficult person with whom you have worked.**

67 Describe the most difficult person with whom you have worked.

- I had a difficult boss at one job—he could be intimidating and impatient—but I learned a lot from him. For example, I learned how to defend my ideas in an assertive but nonaggressive way.

- My former boss was challenging to work with, but I found that gave me incentive to learn and grow so I could deal with her. I found some useful books that helped me understand her contradictory behavior; eventually I got better at anticipating how she would react.

- I had a coworker who was very demanding; I think he was trying to test the boundaries and characters of those around him. I dealt with him by _____ (mention a positive way in which you handled the situation).

- I once worked with someone who was so negative that I found it difficult to be around her. I would try to discuss positive things when I was with her to counterbalance her attitude.

- I have worked with difficult people on occasion who were uncommunicative and did not clearly outline their expectations. I found that the most important thing in those situations is to clarify your objectives and responsibilities.

- So far in my career I have not had to deal with anyone too difficult. However, it is probably only a matter of time before I do. Usually when I encounter difficult people, I try to understand their motives so I can better deal with them.

68 Would you like to sit in my chair one day?

68 Would you like to sit in my chair one day?

- Yes, when my level of expertise matches yours.

- Yes; one of my mid-range goals is to have a job with responsibilities similar to those you have.

- Yes, but only after you have been promoted.

- Not for the time being; maybe one day.

- Yes, if you find another chair that's more comfortable! Seriously, I do aspire to a position like yours. When I get there, and one day I'm interviewing a candidate myself, I'll try to be as _____ as you have been today (mention one or two genuine, positive attributes, such as "gracious and frank" or "welcoming and helpful").

69 How would you characterize your relationships with your colleagues?

69 How would you characterize your relationships with your colleagues?

- Excellent. In the type of work I do, I could not operate without their support and confidence.

- I have strong relationships with them; there's an atmosphere of harmony and respect for one another.

- We know each other well enough to be honest with one another, and the contributions of each person are appreciated.

- Great—they are an inexhaustible source of new ideas and learning opportunities.

- I have always liked working with others. In my last position, I was extremely lucky to be part of a team of bright, dedicated individuals who worked together in a collaborative, egalitarian manner.

- My coworkers turn to me when problems come up because they know I can troubleshoot the problem and find solutions.

- Because of the independent nature of my work, I don't have much regular contact with others. When I do interact with colleagues, I am professional and courteous.

70 **What types of people do you have the most difficulty dealing with?**

70 What types of people do you have the most difficulty dealing with?

- I am flexible and can adapt to most people. However, stubborn people do not inspire or motivate me.

- I prefer to work with people who are open and honest, especially when a situation is difficult.

- I usually don't have trouble getting along with people; that's just my nature. However, it can be tough to have confidence in people who slack off and always make excuses for why their work is incomplete.

- I don't do as well with inflexible, autocratic people as I do with those who are direct and encourage cooperation among group members.

- I prefer working with people who acknowledge and praise others for a job well done rather than those who try to take credit for everything.

71 Can you discuss a time when you had a disagreement with your last boss?

71 Can you discuss a time when you had a disagreement with your last boss?

- We have had lively discussions about strategic viewpoints; however, we usually ended up in agreement once we considered the key factors and understood the possible outcomes.

- We never had one, but if we had, I would have dealt with it by asking questions and trying to understand her point of view.

- I recall one instance in which each of us was arguing for a different solution to a problem. We ended up choosing neither alternative; instead, we agreed on a third one that turned out to be a successful and creative solution.

- I have had conflicts in the past, but they have always been minor. When they happened, it was usually because we hadn't clearly looked into both sides of the situation. When we laid out both perspectives, we were able to reach a compromise.

- Yes, my boss and I disagreed on whether to hire an outside consultant for a project, and I had to convince him of the consultant's value. After I made my case, my boss decided to hire the consultant, who turned out to be very helpful.

- Yes, it was about _____. However, when I couldn't persuade him that my choice was the right one, I ultimately accepted his decision. He was the boss, and I respected his authority.

72 **Describe the best boss you've ever had.**

72 Describe the best boss you've ever had.

- I've gained valuable lessons about work and work relationships from each boss at my last three jobs. For example, _____ (list one lesson that you learned from each former boss).

- My last boss encouraged us to share our ideas with him, and when he liked them, he made sure they were implemented and always gave us credit. For example, I suggested we _____.

- My first boss out of college was encouraging and supportive and kept nudging me toward my goals. She praised my work when I was heading in the right direction and was always there with helpful advice when I felt discouraged.

- My best boss was honest with me—even when I didn't want to hear it. I could always go to him for sincere, frank feedback.

- The best boss I ever had focused more on what I was doing right than what I was doing wrong. Consequently, I worked hard to keep improving. She took the time to discuss my strengths and asked me where I wanted to go in the future.

- My best boss never let me give up or slack off. He knew that I had to be aggressive and keep on learning and growing in order to succeed.

- The best boss I ever had challenged me. She often gave me projects that were a real stretch for me, but she made sure that if I took on the challenge, I could succeed.

73 **If your boss implemented a plan or policy that you strongly disagreed with, what would you do?**

73 If your boss implemented a plan or policy that you strongly disagreed with, what would you do?

- I would let her know my opinion in a constructive way, without being confrontational. I believe it is important to speak up for what you believe.

- I would acknowledge the strong points of his proposal or plan and then suggest that we reexamine it together, offering my suggestions for improvement.

- I would make sure to confirm all my facts before speaking up. Once I was confident that I was speaking from a sound strategic position, I would offer my suggestions in a diplomatic way.

- I felt too intimidated to ever disagree with my first boss. I later realized that it was because we hadn't formed a solid relationship. Since then, I have made a point to establish a strong relationship with every boss, and now I feel confident enough to freely express a difference of opinion.

- If I felt comfortable approaching my boss about this, I would tactfully point out how his approach might adversely affect what he was trying to accomplish. However, each person brings a different point of view to the table, so I would listen to his reasoning for making the decision.

- I would find an opportunity to express my thoughts to my boss privately. I would never bring up this kind of disagreement in front of others.

74 How would you rate the last company you worked for?

74 How would you rate the last company you worked for?

Always answer positively; if the last company you worked for was unsatisfactory, focus on what you learned from the experience.

- My last employer was very professional; the management team always kept things running smoothly and rewarded its employees appropriately. My experience there taught me the value of efficiency, sticking to deadlines, and following through on commitments.

- We parted on good terms. I had a limited-time contract with them, but always felt welcomed and appreciated by my co-workers during my time there.

- My last workplace was a comfortable place to be—well-run, well-equipped, and efficient. I loved working there.

- I continue to have excellent personal and professional relation-ships with many of my former colleagues there.

- I liked working there, but it was a large company so I knew only those in my department well.

75 **How do you deal with office politics?**

75 How do you deal with office politics?

- I try to steer clear of them by staying focused on my job and always documenting my work. That way there can be no misunderstanding down the road about who did what and when.

- I don't gossip, and if I hear it, I remove myself from the conversation. Gossip is hurtful and counterproductive, and spreading gossip is a prime way to get in trouble at the office and lose the respect of your coworkers.

- When things go wrong and I have a valid complaint, I express it though the proper channels. This helps keep the waters clear and avoids unnecessary conflict.

- I always treat my coworkers and superiors with respect, courtesy, and integrity, no matter where they rank in the office hierarchy. That way, if a genuine problem arises, I feel comfortable approaching the appropriate parties or authorities to discuss the issue. Because I have already established myself as a trustworthy individual, they will be more inclined to take my concerns seriously.

- I think it's important to know your own blind spots. I'm careful to be aware of any cliques or factions that form and to understand their motivations. That way I don't intentionally or unintentionally alienate others in the office.

76 Please discuss a career decision you made that was questioned.

76 Please discuss a career decision you made that was questioned.

- When I decided to leave my previous job, my boss tried to change my mind and offered me several incentives to stay. However, I wanted to pursue another job because _____.

- Colleagues tried to persuade me not to pursue my interest in _____ (name the subject or field) because _____. However, I am glad I did because _____.

- I made the decision to move forward on a project and my boss questioned whether I was moving too fast. When I assured him that I had all aspects of the project under control, he accepted my decision.

- As leader of a project, I had final authority for making the decision to _____. Several of my team members questioned my rationale, so I brought them all together to make sure that they understood the reasons for my choice. I believe that when all team members are included and given the pertinent information, they can better understand why certain decisions are made and see the big picture.

- I was responsible for hiring a departmental administrator and chose someone who was less experienced than some of the other candidates. Several of my colleagues questioned my choice, but after I explained why I thought he was the best option, they understood my decision. I'm happy to say that this person exceeded expectations and is still with the company.

77 Why do you think communication is important at work?

77 Why do you think communication is important at work?

- Communication is a critical factor for progress and success; I've found that the quality of anyone's work is proportional to their ability to communicate.

- Frequent communication—exchanging and sharing information—plays a major role in all kinds of continuous learning. It helps keep everyone well informed and fosters a feeling of understanding and inclusion.

- Honest communication—that means people saying what they mean and meaning what they say—is really the lifeblood of a company. When people conceal or withhold their real opinions and intentions, it creates mistrust and confusion and can sabotage the best plans.

- Without clear communication, it's easy for problems to arise and to make mistakes that could have been avoided. Directions and expectations always need to be explicit to prevent potential conflict and to maximize productivity.

- Clear communication is essential in interactions between colleagues, particularly when key information or instructions are being transmitted. I like to write things down whenever possible, as it helps me make sure that what I'm trying to say is specific and understandable.

78 What is your teamwork style?

78 What is your teamwork style?

- I am a team player, and I often take the initiative to lead a group because I'm highly motivated, focused, and confident in my leadership abilities. I ask a lot of questions to make sure everyone is on the same page, and am careful never to seem bossy or unreceptive to new ideas.

- I am very focused on the project at hand and can bring the group members back to the task if we get off track. I want to make sure that the job gets done as thoroughly and efficiently as possible.

- I am a person who values teamwork; I thrive on keeping the peace. I like cooperation, listening to other's suggestions, and working by consensus.

- I am an idea person and enjoy challenges. I encourage others to take on new and different projects and to find new ways to overcome problems.

- I am highly organized and like keeping the group moving at a steady pace. I value logic and systematic thinking.

- I find that I'm most efficient when I connect with my team periodically—by email, at meetings, or by dropping by each other's offices.

- Since I am fairly new to the job market, I really enjoy being part of a team. I'm eager to learn from those with more experience and to contribute my own ideas, which can offer a fresh perspective because I'm not yet entrenched in the work culture.

79 What was the outcome of your last performance evaluation?

79 What was the outcome of your last performance evaluation?

- Excellent; it was a positive, constructive exchange with my boss. She confirmed that I had reached my goals, including _____ and _____.

- Overall it was very good. It was a great opportunity to get some helpful feedback. I did realize that I could strengthen my skills in _____ to do an even better job in the future.

- I was not happy with it. I realized that my boss and I needed to improve our communication, as I learned that I had not understood all of the expectations she had for me.

- Very good. My boss said that I had _____ (mention two or three of your strongest accomplishments or skills that your boss commended).

- My boss thought that I had not done as well as I could have in the area of _____. I understood that there was room for improvement, so I have made a considerable effort to work on this by _____.

80 Why are you looking for a job?

80 Why are you looking for a job?

- I have worked at my last job for X years and believe my skills and abilities have grown in that time, but there is no further room for advancement there. I want to find another job that is better suited to my current level of competence.

- My present job no longer matches my aspirations and goals; I hope to _____ (mention two or three objectives that match those of the job you're applying for).

- I am making a career change and wish to offer my services to a company that _____ (give one or two distinctive features of the company you hope to join).

- With so many jobs being outsourced to Asia, I watched many of my colleagues lose their jobs and decided that I needed to proactively look for another job. I've always been interested in _____ (name the field of the position you're applying for); in fact, it was my first major in college before I switched to _____. That's why I started to prepare myself for this position.

- I always wanted a job that involved travel (or "working at night; I do my best work then"), but for my kids' sake I didn't pursue that until they were grown. Now I'm free to follow that dream.

- Just like countless others, I was let go because of the recent downturn in the economy. For financial reasons out of my control, my entire department/team was dissolved, even though we had many competent and accomplished employees.

81 Why have you been unemployed for so long?

81 Why have you been unemployed for so long?

- I took time to polish my knowledge in _____ (name an appropriate and relevant area, such as a particular technology or foreign language).

- I needed some time to do a thorough self-assessment. Now everything is clear to me, and I'm eager to rejoin the workforce.

- I carefully study the job offers I receive and consider only those that will allow me to do meaningful, quality work.

- I am making a radical career change, and that takes time. I am now at the stage where I know exactly what I am looking for; I contacted you because this job offers just that.

- Finding just any job is not too difficult, but finding the right job takes persistence and time.

- The job market has been a difficult one for quite a while—I network with other job-seekers, and they concur that it's tough and takes a lot of effort and patience. I've been active and diligent in my job search; it just takes longer to find the right opportunity—like this one.

82 Why did you quit your last job?

82 Why did you quit your last job?

- My professional knowledge was not used to its fullest there. I think your company and this job provide a greater opportunity to contribute all that I have to offer.

- Before my last job, I had always worked in very stimulating work environments where I could commit myself wholeheartedly. I eventually realized this wasn't going to happen if I remained in that position.

- My department was going to be eliminated for strategic and budgetary reasons.

- I received a promotion that did not match my goals. They offered me a staff position, but I believe I am better suited for a management position because _____.

- My company went through a downsizing recently, and I knew that I needed to move on, to keep my morale up and to keep my skills on the cutting edge.

- I was looking for ways to enhance and expand my technical skills, and I knew that my former job would not give me that important opportunity.

- The company's management approach didn't match my own work style, and despite numerous attempts at reconciliation, our methodologies just weren't compatible. Instead of trying to fit into a system that I wasn't comfortable with, I decided that the best option would be to move on and find another job.

83 Why do you want to work for us?

83 **Why do you want to work for us?**

- The position and the company's mission match my objectives exactly: _____ (mention two or three objectives that you have in common).

- Your company has a reputation for excellence, and I believe that I can actively contribute to your success in the future.

- I have been in situations similar to those you now face; I'm confident that my skills and experience will be useful here.

- I can offer your company _____, _____, and _____ (describe three positive contributions you can make that will be valuable to this particular employer).

- I have admired your company for quite some time and have kept myself up-to-date on your products/services. I am particularly attracted to _____ (describe what most interests you).

- I have studied your company and your competitors quite thoroughly, and I believe that my understanding of this market would make a valuable contribution.

84 What is the status of your job hunt?

84 What is the status of your job hunt?

Always be honest about your status. Do not say that you have received job offers unless this is genuinely the case. Even if you haven't made much progress or received any offers, you can still present this to the interviewer in a positive light.

- I am optimistic. I've completed the first phase: gathering and analyzing information. I have just launched the second phase: approaching organizations and scheduling interviews.

- I am doing well. I have established contacts with four companies, including yours. Negotiations are progressing with two of them, but I am still uncommitted, and it's prudent for me to keep pursuing other attractive prospects.

- It's going well. I have received two job offers and will soon face the difficult task of deciding whether to choose one of them, or—if your company makes me an offer—to join this team.

- I have been in contact with my network and see some promising leads on the horizon.

- I am busy at my job hunt every day and have identified some terrific resources. Thanks to these, I expect to find a job within six weeks.

85 Have you approached other organizations?

85 Have you approached other organizations?

Always be honest about your contact—or lack thereof—with other organizations. Do not say that you have approached other companies if you have not.

- Not yet. This job offers me exactly what I want to do, something no other company can offer. I promised myself I'd focus on this opportunity until a decision is made.

- Not yet; I am just starting my job search and believe this position would be a great fit for me.

- Yes, two others as of now. Both are interesting companies, but this position is my first choice.

- Yes, _____ and _____. Perhaps you can give me an industry insider's perspective on how they compare to your company?

- Yes, two others. One has offered me an interview next week, and I'm expecting to hear back from the other shortly.

86 Why should I hire you instead of someone else?

86 Why should I hire you instead of someone else?

- This is such an appealing position, I'm sure you have other candidates who are as interested in it as I am. I believe my strength lies in what I have to offer: _____ (summarize your key qualifications).

- I am extremely enthusiastic and my skills match the required tasks: _____ (list three).

- I believe my personality is a great fit for this company and I have the experience and capabilities you seek. (List three.)

- Your company and I share the same objectives: _____ (name two or three). This would be a mutually beneficial relationship, allowing us both to realize our potential.

- I know that I may not have as much experience as some of the other candidates for this job, but I can offer _____ and _____ (name two strong personality traits or characteristics and provide two accomplishments to illustrate them).

87 **If I were to make you a firm job offer, what would your answer be?**

87 If I were to make you a firm job offer, what would your answer be?

- I would ask you to give me some time to reflect.

- I would be delighted to discuss it; first, however, would you please let me know just a little more about _____ (name any areas where you might still need some clarification: the job tasks/responsibilities, working conditions, and so on, but do not ask about salary).

- I would be thrilled, and I think we would have no problem agreeing on the specifics.

- I would thank you for your trust in me and be honored to join your company. I believe you will be happy to have me working for you.

- I would accept, provided that we could work out the details to be mutually satisfactory.

88 Have you gotten any job offers?

88 Have you gotten any job offers?

Always be honest about this. Even if you haven't received any offers, you can still present this to the interviewer in a positive light.

- I've had three promising interviews in the last month with interesting companies, so I'm optimistic.

- I'm still waiting for answers from other companies, so no, not quite yet.

- A headhunter contacted me with some possible positions that might be a good fit, so I'm definitely making progress in my job search.

- I have contacted very few companies—only those that really match what I'm looking for. Because I'm very clear about that, it does narrow my choices. That's one reason I was particularly excited to learn about this opening.

- Yes, I've had a few offers, but everything is still open. This job is my first choice, because _____ (name two or three aspects of the job that appeal to you).

- Not yet; I just began my job search and am starting with the job I want most.

89 How will you decide which job offer to take, including ours?

89 How will you decide which job offer to take, including ours?

An interviewer will usually ask this only if you have stated that you have received other offers. Never claim that you have received job offers when you, in fact, have not.

- I will take yours with enthusiasm! I believe this job is the best match for me.

- I will weigh the merits of the three jobs I have been offered and figure out which company would be the best fit for my skills and abilities. My goal is to work with a company where I can build a career, not just take a job.

- My decision is already 90 percent in your favor. May I have forty-eight hours to confirm it?

- Your organization offers two very positive points: _____ and _____. May I take the night to think over your offer?

- I would love to accept an offer from you, but before doing so, I would like to work out a few details so that your offer meets or exceeds those that I've received from other companies. Is this something you would consider?

90 We're just about done. Do you have any questions to ask me?

90 We're just about done. Do you have any questions to ask me?

Always ask at least one question; your curiosity will show the interviewer that you are interested, thorough, and inquisitive. Do not, however, ask about something that has already been covered in depth or something that you should have researched beforehand.

- Yes, thank you. I would like to know more about _____ (name one or two aspects of the job or company).

- We've covered the basic questions well today. I'm hoping that I make the first cut and that you will invite me back to talk more about the specifics. Do you have any sense about that at this point? (If the interviewer answers positively, ask "Who should take the initiative for the next contact?")

- Yes, I do. May I ask what conclusion you have come to after this interview?

- Yes. What do you hope the person who takes this job will do that the person formerly in the job did not?

- Yes. Could you tell me a little about yourself, how long you have been here, and what drew you to this company?

- Thank you. I'd like to know whether the person who held this position was promoted or left the company.

- Yes. What do you consider to be the single most challenging aspect of this job?

#4

CONCERN #4:
WHAT WILL YOU COST US?

How much will hiring and employing you cost the company?

What do I need to offer in order to get you?

What are you willing to trade off in order to work here?

91 **What was your last salary?**

91 What was your last salary?

- My last salary was within the range that I'm now looking for, which is between $X and $Y (mention a fairly broad range).

- I'm sorry, but I can't share this information yet. My employer and I have an agreement that forbids me from discussing my salary outside the company. If we decide that I'm the right person for the job, I'm sure we can negotiate a fair salary.

- My salary is a topic that I would be happy to discuss after I have received a job offer. Have we reached a point where you are ready to make me a firm offer?

- This position has several key differences from my last job. So before we determine a fair salary, can we discuss the responsibilities of the job in greater detail?

- My salary was consistent with the contribution I made to my last employer. (If the interviewer asks three times for you to name a figure, give a range that includes your last salary.)

92 Are you willing to lower your salary expectation?

92 Are you willing to lower your salary expectation?

- It depends how much you need me to lower it.

- Yes. (Remain completely quiet for at least eight seconds, which will often force the interviewer to say more and reveal what he or she is thinking.)

- Yes, if the salary is adjusted upward after a specified time period that we negotiate now.

- Yes, if it's possible for me to be compensated with other non-salary benefits.

- If the work environment is good and there are strong possibilities for promotion, I would consider it.

- Possibly, if we can revise the job description accordingly. I'd consider accepting a lower figure if I'm able to be more selective in my duties and projects.

- I would love to be in a position to negotiate a lower salary; however, it is just not possible at this time due to my current financial obligations. (Warning: Answering in this way may be a risk—be aware that you may jeopardize your chances of getting the job. Nonetheless, do not agree to a lower salary if you will not be able to pay your bills. In the long run, you are better off continuing to search for a job that provides a salary sufficient for your economic needs.)

93 How did you justify your salary in your last job?

93 How did you justify your salary in your last job?

- Very simply, I was paid on a commission basis: if I produced results, my salary reflected that.

- My targets were very clear, and I worked overtime to meet them when necessary.

- I did my job with enthusiasm and took my responsibilities very seriously. I succeeded in _____ (mention one or two achievements that illustrate your value to the company).

- By generating results in company revenue that were X times the size of my salary.

- I saved the company a considerable amount of money by negotiating new vendor contracts and identifying and eliminating wasteful spending. I was able to compile concrete numbers to show my boss how much I was saving the company each month.

- I am very good at what I do, and I'm always willing to go the extra mile. For example, _____.

94 At this stage in your career, why aren't you earning a higher salary?

94 At this stage in your career, why aren't you earning a higher salary?

- My previous job was radically different from the one we are now discussing; the salary ranges are lower across the board in that industry. It's a very creative field to be in, so most workers consider it worth the financial sacrifice, but I realize now that I need to seek more financial security.

- Money has never been my primary motivation in a job. Throughout my career, what's been most important to me is doing work I really enjoy for a company I respect.

- My previous salary did not reflect all of my additional benefits and total compensation package, which had significant value.

- I took time out from my career to pursue other interests, knowing that I would likely suffer some in the salary area. This was my choice, and I was willing to accept the consequences.

- I believe I am worth more than I am currently making; this is one reason I am looking for a new job.

- I am fortunate to be in a position in which I don't need to make money the primary motivating factor for accepting a job.

95 What are you worth?

95 What are you worth?

- My career path is important to me, and I don't base decisions about its direction primarily on financial concerns. Perhaps I can address this question after we have discussed my qualifications and experience further.

- Thank you for bringing this up; before we discuss this, could you please elaborate on the following job responsibilities so I am sure that I understand everything the job entails? (Name one or two that you would like to discuss further.)

- I believe I am worth $X because: _____ (name three ways in which you can actively contribute to the company).

- I am confident that I am worth the top of the range, because I've proven that I can produce results. For example, _____.

- I've been in this field for X years, and I've researched the typical salary range for this job in our area. On that basis, I think a range between $Y and $Z corresponds to the value of my work.

96 What salary figure do you have in mind?

96 What salary figure do you have in mind?

- I am looking to earn a salary that is commensurate with my potential and future contribution.

- I would like to be making between $X and $Y within three to five years.

- I am interested in the range of $X and $Y; we can narrow this down once I have more information about the job.

- My research suggests a range between $X and $Y, and I believe my skills and experience position me in the top of the range.

- At this stage, before giving you a definitive answer I would need more information about the job to accurately assess my value to the department/company.

- I think it would be helpful to our discussion if I understood what your company considers an appropriate salary for this job. Do you have a range in mind?

97 Would you be willing to accept a lower salary for a training period of six months?

97 Would you be willing to accept a lower salary for a training period of six months?

- Is a training period at reduced salary a standard requirement for new hires, or is there a particular reason you want me to consider it?

- The idea of improving myself and learning new techniques interests me a lot. Could you please describe the training?

- I am very interested in this job. Could we discuss this point later when we have covered the key responsibilities of the job?

- What additional responsibilities would I have after this initial training period?

- I would consider it, but because I am a very fast learner, I'd like to know whether the length of the training period could be determined by my progress and shortened if I came up to speed more rapidly than anticipated.

- I am not sure I could accept such an arrangement. I believe in myself and my abilities and feel I am worth the full salary. (Warning: Answering in this way may be a risk—be aware that you may jeopardize your chances of getting the job.)

98 What kind of benefits are you looking for?

98 What kind of benefits are you looking for?

- Comprehensive medical and dental insurance are the most important benefits to me.

- I am interested pursuing additional training in _____ (name the subject or field). Do you offer any type of tuition reimbursement for continuing education or specific training courses?

- I am interested in the standard benefits that most companies offer. I would be happy to negotiate these once we reach an agreement that I am the right person for the job.

- I have done my research and see that you offer a good benefit package. This gives me confidence that I'd be satisfied with that part of the compensation.

- As this job involves a considerable amount of local travel, I would be interested in discussing the use of a company car and mileage reimbursement.

99 How important is salary to you?

99 How important is salary to you?

- While salary is of course important to me, it's just one factor in choosing a job. I want to make a difference in my work and collaborate with compatible people on tasks I enjoy. This means more to me than the amount of financial compensation.

- Salary is important, and so far in my career I have always received a salary that fairly corresponded to my contribution. I hope this will be the case in the future as well.

- I appreciate a good salary as a sign that my work is valued.

- Money is important, but fulfillment is even more so. I look for jobs that match my skills and abilities, not only those that only offer a high salary.

- I would rank salary among the top five things that matter most to me about this job. However, it's certainly not number one.

100 How do you feel about working overtime?

100 How do you feel about working overtime?

- If it is essential to getting the task done, I can always make room in my schedule.

- I have no problem with reasonable overtime. How are these hours compensated?

- I am happy to work until the job is done.

- Is the company open to having employees do some or all of the overtime work from home?

- Perhaps we could work out a way to avoid overtime.

- It would depend on the extent and frequency. In theory, I would say yes now; in practice, I hope the company would recognize the need for employees to have a fair balance between work and family.

- Yes, of course, as long as it isn't a routine expectation, but an exception for a good reason, like a project deadline.

101 **What do you expect to be earning in five years?**

101 What do you expect to be earning in five years?

- In five years, I would say 15 to 20 percent more than I do now.

- In five years, I expect I will have developed my skills and acquired the experience to have earned several promotions, with the accompanying increase in salary.

- I expect to be making in the neighborhood of $X to $Y (mention a range).

- As I'm just beginning my career, it makes sense to expect that I will be making considerably more in five years, but I wouldn't venture to predict a specific figure.

- Working in this field allows me to dream big—I would say 50 percent more than I make now.

ABOUT THE AUTHORS

A leading pioneer for more than thirty years in career design and job hunting, **Daniel Porot** is an internationally recognized career expert. Daniel received his MBA in 1966 from the Business School of France, Insead, and began his career with Exxon and Amoco before starting his own business in 1971.

He has authored more than fifteen best-selling French-language career books, translated Richard N. Bolles's *What Color Is Your Parachute?* into French, and written *The Pie Method for Career Success* and *101 Salary Secrets* for U.S. audiences. Daniel has personally trained more than eleven thousand job hunters and six hundred career counselors, and his training materials have been used by over one million job hunters worldwide. Daniel also taught an annual two-week workshop with Richard Bolles for more than twenty years. He lives in Geneva, Switzerland, with his wife and has four children.

Visit www.porot.com

Frances Bolles Haynes has worked in the field of career development for more than twenty-five years. She began her career in Phoenix, Arizona, helping participants in Comprehensive Employment and Training Act (CETA) programs find employment. She then moved to Jackson, Mississippi, where she set up a successful job-hunting program based on the Job Club model, pioneered by Nathan Azrin.

She is a longtime colleague of Daniel Porot and has coauthored four books with him. For several years, they wrote a weekly column for the *Wall Street Journal* on career issues. She also served on the training staff of Richard Bolles. She is thankful to them both for their wisdom and genius. Frances lives in Newport Beach, California, with her husband, Peter, and son, Donald.

WITHDRAWN